MASTERPIECES FROM THE GREAT

DUTCH MUSEUMS

MASTERPIECES FROM THE GREAT

DUTCH
MUSEUMS

RIJKSMUSEUM · MAURITSHUIS
BOYMANS-VAN BEUNINGEN
FRANS HALS MUSEUM

BY

R. VAN LUTTERVELT

Curator, Department of History, Rijksmuseum, Amsterdam

HARRY N. ABRAMS, INC · PUBLISHERS · NEW YORK

CONTENTS

THE EARLIEST COLLECTIONS

The earliest collections of rare, strange and beautiful objects were formed in the treasure vaults of medieval churches. In these were kept relics of the saints in handsomely worked reliquaries made of silver and studded with precious stones, books in costly ornamented bindings, valuable chalices, monstrances, paraments and oblations. On feast days all these beautiful things were exhibited on the altars, as can be seen, for instance, on the dedicatory-miniature in a manuscript from the Abbey of Egmond, made in the middle of the tenth century, which is now in the Royal Library at The Hague. Apart from relics, reliquaries, Bibles and other books, the treasure vaults of medieval churches also contained rarities of a not strictly religious nature, such as great narwhal teeth which were then thought to be the horns of unicorns, fabulous animals, part horse, part antelope, with one horn in the middle of their forehead and a reputation for holiness. Public opinion attributed magic strength to these horns, which made them coveted possessions. Among the church treasures one even found statuettes of idols from the heathen past, because of their curiosity (so it was said), but who is to say whether somewhere, deep down in the subconsciousness of the people, there was not a hidden feeling that, despite Christianity, these idols could not be entirely trusted and it was better to give them an honourable place within the walls of a consecrated building?

The Reformation in the Netherlands led to the destruction of the greater part of these extraordinary collections, but those at Maastricht, Oldenzaal and those of the five Chapters of Utrecht were saved.

The latter were probably among the most remarkable in this field in the Netherlands. They did not come to the State until 1811 and, as a result, what was left eventually found its way into the Rijksmuseum – precious silverwork, unicorns, ivory and leather boxes, figures of saints and bronze statuettes of idols, a sabre and more of the like.

Despite the great diversity of objects, no paintings were included in the treasuries of the medieval churches. The custom of making movable paintings on panels did not originate until some time in the fourteenth century. As a result of the Iconoclasm of the sixteenth century and the destructive war that followed it—in which even the Spanish soldiers sometimes wrought havoc in the churches—not much is left in the Northern Netherlands of the triptychs and other paintings which from that period began to adorn the altars. Some treasures were taken to safety in time. Most of these were lost sight of soon after and when, after centuries of wandering, they at last reached our museums, their adventures could only be reconstructed to a very limited extent.

This is the case with Geertgen tot Sint Jans' *Tree of Jesse* (p. 274), which must have been painted for the Church of the White Sisters at Haarlem, or of the triptych of *The Dance round the Golden Calf* (pp. 104–5) by Lucas van Leyden (both now in the Rijksmuseum). One or two other works of art, such as the painting of *Mary with Child surrounded by Four Female Saints* (p. 91) by the anonymous painter of Delft (who owes to this painting his name 'Master of the Virgo inter Virgines') seem to have been stored with the archives of the Convents for which they were painted, and thus to have been saved. A fragment of the great, much-admired altar of Pieter Aertsz from the New Church in Amsterdam (p. 125) was preserved, thanks to the quality of the work. The municipal government took care of it and had it taken to the town hall.

Thus art-loving governors in the Netherlands were able occasionally to save important pieces from destruction or disappearance. In the great artistic centre of Haarlem, however, not a single medieval ecclesiastical painting it left, nor is there one in The Hague or Rotterdam.

On their removal from a church to the town hall or to a collector's cabinet the paintings changed their purpose: from being objects of religious worship they became objects of artistic admiration, collector's pieces, in fact.

The collecting of paintings started later than the habit of gathering holy, curious or rare objects. Such collections only began to be made during the Renaissance and to a certain extent they imitated the older ecclesiastical treasuries and secular cabinets of curiosities. This applies to the Netherlands as well as to the rest of Europe. Only when the art of panel-painting had definitely acquired its own forms and own rights of existence did it become suitable for use not merely in churches but also in private houses and for secular purposes. Thus collections of paintings began to be formed, for various reasons. Some collections, mainly of portraits, were brought together out of historical interest or family pride; some were mixed collections which merely served to decorate the house, to please the eye or as a show of prosperity; some were made simply to satisfy a passion for collecting.

GROUP-PORTRAITS OF CIVIC GUARDS, AND GOVERNING BODIES, AND OTHER WORKS FROM PUBLIC INSTITUTIONS

As early as the Middle Ages, military service was demanded from able-bodied townsmen. This is already mentioned in early fourteenth century Amsterdam documents. The Civic Guards which these men formed eventually expanded into guilds, bodies of importance in the town. They possessed their own buildings, the 'Doelen' (literally: butts). Amsterdam had three which were called after the arms carried by the companies; the Long-bow Doelen, the Cross-bow Doelen and, most important of all, the 'Kloveniersdoelen' for those using muskets with 'kloven' or 'kolven' (butt-ends).

The command of the Civic Guards was in the hands of the burgo-master of the town. The principal officers under him also usually belonged to the ruling class. It was considered an honour to be in the Civic Guard and it was specifically laid down members should dress and arm themselves at their own expense, which they did as well as they could afford, each according to his own taste. Uniform dress for military personnel did not exist at that time. At most the guardsmen of a company wore the same sashes to distinguish them from other groups. With the change in military tactics and the advent of artillery in the sixteenth century, the importance of military service for the population of the towns decreased. By and by their task came to be, almost exclusively, that of patrolling and closing the streets for state visits and other special occasions. But the appearance of the gentle-men was not less colourful as a result. The social gatherings and the banquets that went with them became increasingly important and so did the Doelen buildings. Their big halls came to be among the finest and most impressive in the town, on account of the exquisite group-portraits that were hung there.

Portrait-groups of the Civic Guards have only been painted in Holland and Zeeland. The genre arose in Amsterdam, during the city's first period of prosperity. The basis for this form of art had, however, been prepared in Haarlem by Geertgen tot Sint Jans whose altar wing with the portraits of the *Knights of St John* (Kunsthistorisches Museum, Vienna) is considered to be the oldest Dutch group-portrait. A generation later Jan van Scorel, in his panels of Utrecht and Haarlem, *Pilgrims to Jerusalem* (see p. 276, where it is titled Crusaders at Haarlem), had further elaborated the theme. Therefore, the idea of painting men in a group existed already. What was new, however, was that they did not have themselves painted for a religious purpose but for purely municipal or civic reasons. In fact it was in Amsterdam that the group-portrait became secularised. The subject was to have great vitality.

The first Civic Guard's piece is the triptych-shaped panel painted by Dirck Jacobsz in 1529 as a commission by the officers of the Kloveniersdoelen. No one has recorded what inspired those citizens of Amsterdam when they proudly had their portraits made, in an ostentatious manner, such as princes and noblemen had not until then been accustomed to. Of the relationship between those first patrons and the artist who had to carry out the work we know nothing. The curious thing is that this became an established practice even before Calvinism and Iconoclasm deprived religious painters of their living by banning paintings from the Northern-Netherlandish churches, a generation before Dutchmen were to abjure their monarch and form a republic. Painter and patrons were thus considerably ahead of the political, historical and religious developments.

The new subject immediately became popular, and in rapid succession other Guards' pieces were painted in 1531, in 1532, then in 1533 the *Banquet of the Civic Guard of Amsterdam* (p. 277) – the first of its kind – by Cornelis Anthonisz. The series, once started, was continued through the following decades and in the seventeenth century developed into a grandiose succession of exceedingly sizeable canvases. The largest commissions for the painting of Guards' pieces were given in the years 1638 or 1639 to 1643 during the installation of the new hall of the Amsterdam 'Kloveniers' in the Nieuwe Doelenstraat, where today the Doelen Hotel stands. The paintings created in this short period were never surpassed. The first, completed in 1640, was by Joachim Sandrart who recorded in it the State Visit of the Queen of France, Marie de Medici, in 1638. Other groups of Civic Guards were painted for the hall by Jacob Backer, Nicolaes Elias, Govert Flinck, Bartholomeus van der Helst and, the most outstanding by far, Rembrandt's painting of the company of Frans Banningh Cocq which, incorrectly titled *The Nightwatch* (p. 184–5) became world-famous.

The example of the new Kloveniersdoelen was followed by the Amsterdam Long-bow Doelen. In 1645 Nicolaes Elias completed for their hall his picture of the company of Captain Jacob Rogh, while Van der Helst created for it his colossal masterpiece, a *Banquet* (p. 294) showing Captain Cornelis Janszoon Witsen and his men celebrating the Peace of Westphalia in 1648. Captain Johan Huydecoper, not to be outdone, commissioned Govert Flinck in the same year to depict in a group-painting how his company had celebrated the conclusion of the peace. It appears symbolic that this was to be the last full-length Guards' piece.

It was customary that they should not be paid for out of municipal funds or from the general treasury of the Civic Guard; each person paid for his own portrait. We know, for example, that for Rembrandt's *Nightwatch* those portrayed spent on the average about one hundred guilders each for their picture, one a little more, another less, depending on the place they occupied on the canvas. Once hung in the Doelen, the Guards' pieces automatically became the property of the Civic Guard–a municipal organisation in fact. Thus, without further formality, they became the property of the town, which they have remained until the present day. Those of Amsterdam were transferred after the abolition of the Doelen in the eighteenth century, to the small and the large Court-Martial Chambers of the town hall. Right from the beginning they became a spectacle of the first order.

The Civic Guard of Haarlem was organised on the same footing as that of Amsterdam. A document of 1402 in the municipal archives mentions the official recognition of a company of 120 guardsmen. Their armaments consisted of long-bows. They had taken as their patron saint the knightly St George and had their headquarters in the Doelen near the Grote Houtpoort. The building dated from 1591 and still exists, although in a changed condition.

Whereas the men of St George belonged to the élite of the town, those of St Sebastian, who used the cross-bow, sprang from the ordinary population. The company did not play an important part in the life of Haarlem, and in 1560 ceased to exist. The development of firearms had in the meantime made it necessary for the Civic Guards to be trained in their use as well. In 1519, therefore, a third organisation was founded, that of the Kloveniers, dedicated to St Adrian. Their Doelen building in the Gasthuisstraat dates mainly from 1562. This, too, the visitor to Haarlem can still find, albeit no longer in its former glory. A reorganisation, which was completed in 1560, brought the Civic Guards – now only those of St George and St Adrian – directly under the local magistrate. In 1558, on the initiative of the municipal government, it had already been decided that once a year, on the occasion of the transfer of posts, a banquet or repast would be given at the expense of the town. In the past, too, after a shooting match, the guards had dined together but it was then customary for participants to bring their own food. But now the reunion was not restricted to one dinner. From an ordinance of 1633 it appears that the occasion had been extended to cover a whole week and that as a result heavy demands were made on the funds of the municipal treasury!

The arrangement of 1558 therefore soon became a popular tradition and one of outstanding historical importance, for it was here that Frans Hals found inspiration for the great *Repasts* (pp. 148–9 and 284) which he painted with such a dazzling brush, like no one else before him or since. But he was not the originator of the subject which, as we have already seen, was begun three-quarters of a century earlier by Cornelis Anthonisz of Amsterdam. Frans Hals was not the only Haarlem painter of this sort of group-painting. Before him, Cornelis Cornelisz of Haarlem twice depicted the officers of the Civic Guard at table, in 1583 and in 1599. During Hals' life his fellow-townsmen Cornelis Engelsz and Pieter Claesz Soutman were each commissioned once, in 1618 and 1644 respectively, Frans Pieter Grebber three times – twice in 1619 – and Hendrick Pot once, in 1630. But none of them was able to portray his subjects with such matchless skill, in such light and fierce, gay colours as was Hals. He shows them at laden tables covered with costly damask, relaxed in attitude, and assured in their prosperity and position. Just as in Amsterdam all

14

these paintings automatically became the property of the city, here too they were exhibited in the town hall after the abolition of the Civic Guards. And, as in Amsterdam, they rightly attracted great admiration. It was in the first place to see the Hals pictures that many a fellow-countryman and foreigner travelled to Haarlem.

Various groups of officers of the Rotterdam Civic Guards had themselves portrayed likewise. In 1682 the Doelen of St George possessed no fewer than seventeen paintings. Through neglect these have unfortunately perished with the exception of one, a painting of 1604, by an artist who did not sign his work and whose identity has not yet been rescued from anonymity.

The example set by the Civic Guards' Doelen with their choice group-portraits was followed by various Dutch charitable institutions and guilds. Just as in the case of the Civic Guards, the towns' art collections were enriched inestimably by exquisite paintings of various governing bodies. Outstanding in this series, of course, is Rembrandt's *Syndics* (p. 197), directly followed by Ferdinand Bol's group of four *Governors of the Lepers' Asylum* painted in 1649 and his three respectable and portly *Lady Governors of the Amsterdam Lepers' House*, of 1668. Then follow Nicolaes Maes' six *Wardens of the Guild of Surgeons, Amsterdam,* Karel Dujardin's stately, cool group of the *Spinning House Governors,* of 1669, and the older canvas, of 1628, by Nicolaes Elias showing earlier governors of the same institution.

With the pictures of four *Governors* and three *Lady Governors of the Amsterdam Lepers' House* (p. 293) which Werner van den Valckert painted in 1624, may be mentioned three panels by the same master, on which one sees *Governors of the Orphanage for the Poor*. To this genre belong, moreover, the two remarkable *Anatomy Lessons* by Rembrandt (Mauritshuis and Rijksmuseum) and by Thomas de Keyser (Rijksmuseum).

In other towns of Holland, also, group-portraits of governors became in demand. In Haarlem it began in 1641 with Frans Hals' *Governors of the St Elisabeth's Hospital* (p. 284), in which the Amsterdam tradition of Rembrandt and Thomas de Keyser was followed. At the end of his life Hals painted two more of these: the unequalled *Governors* and *Lady Governors of the Old Men's Home* (p. 285) of 1664. The group-portrait at Haarlem then enjoyed its greatest period. Some years previously, in 1642, Johannes Verspronck had painted *The Governors of the House of the Holy Ghost*. He was followed, in 1658 and 1659, by Jacob van Loo with his *Governors* and *Lady Governors of the Poor House*. In 1663 Jan de Bray painted *The Governors of the Poor Children's Home* (p. 283) to which in 1664 he added the group of lady governors; three years later he once again carried out similar commissions for the *Governors* and *Lady Governors of the Lepers' Asylum*. Somewhat later, in 1674, the *Lady Governors of the House of the Holy Ghost* were painted by Pieter Anraadt, while finally, as late as the eighteenth century, in 1737, Frans Decker immortalised the *Governors of the St Joris* or the *Grote Provenhuis* in all their respectability, gathered round a table.

Among these many group-portraits the painters themselves did not wish to be outdone and in 1675 a lively picture of their own guild *The Wardens of St Luke at Haarlem* (p. 32) was painted. They are grouped round a table, on which a bust in terracotta has been placed; this looks like a portrait of Rembrandt but was probably a sculpture attributed at the time to Michelangelo which the guild had in its possession. The canvas was painted by Jan de Bray who himself was then a Warden. There is a tradition connected with the piece that Dirck de Bray supposedly assisted in its painting by portraying his brother Jan, while Jan painted Dirck, and other artists also collaborated over the canvas. From the results of a recent investigation this story appears to be plausible. Such a complicated history of origin could only be found in a group-portrait of the painters' guild.

Initially the painting must have hung in the wardens' room but, exceptionally, it did not become the property of the town. At the end of the eighteenth century it was in the collection of the Haarlem

Portrait of William I, Prince of Orange, probably 1578,
by Adriaen Thomasz Key (1544–after 1589).
Wood. 48×35 cm. (18⁷/₈″×13³/₄″). Rijksmuseum No. 1336 A 1.

16

artist Wybrand Hendriks. On 16th July 1819 it was auctioned in the famous room of the House with the Heads (on the Keizersgracht) in Amsterdam. Two years later the Rijksmuseum bought this important piece from the broker J. de Vries.

Elsewhere in Holland, also, governors' portraits were painted in the seventeenth century, but not in such great numbers as in Amsterdam and Haarlem, and they were not by any means of the same artistic quality. In 1653 Jan Daemensz Cool of Rotterdam devoted himself to a group of *Governors of the Old Men's Home*. Formerly the town possessed more of them but they have been lost.

The governors of the hospitals and other charitable institutions of the old Dutch towns liked yet another sort of decoration for the institutions under their management, namely paintings with suitable biblical scenes or other religious matter such as *The Good Samaritan, The Works of Charity*, or *The Wedding Guest without Wedding Raiment*. Thus originated in 1628 in Haarlem Pieter Fransz de Grebber's large canvas showing *The Works of Charity* (p. 285) for the Old Men's Home. This institution also possessed an elegant, organ-playing *St Cecilia* by Peter de Witte (Pietro Candido), a scene of *Workers in the Vineyard* by Cornelis Holsteyn, a *Female Singer* by Gerard Honthorst and the painting of a man with a collecting box surrounded by children, by the hand of Cornelis Engelsz. Its halls were further decorated with some topographical views of Haarlem by Vincent Lourentsz van der Vinne (died 1729) and even a painting of the Forum of Nerva in Rome which is attributed to Jacob van der Ulft.

The old Elizabeth's Hospital had, apart from the great group of governors by Frans Hals, yet another work, a late one, by Maerten van Heemskerck, representing *The Good Samaritan* (1568); a *Landscape with the Annunciation* by Abraham Bloemaert; a *Juda and Thamar* by Cornelis Cornelisz of Haarlem (of 1598) and a *Woman playing the Clarinet* by Dirck Hals. In the Heilige Geesthuis one could see a painting of *Christ blessing the Children*, by Cornelis Cornelisz (of 1632); in the Lepers' House was a scene, *Pestilence and Madness* in which the prophet Elijah declines presents offered to him by Naaman, painted by Pieter Fransz de Grebber in 1637; in the

Barbara Hospital various religious representations; in the municipal pawnshop a remarkable work by Job Berckheyde representing *Joseph's Brothers in Egypt* (of 1669), and in the Home of the Knights of Saint John, besides three panels with Pilgrims to Jerusalem by Jan van Scorel, his colourful *Baptism of Christ in the River Jordan* and his *Adam and Eve*. Moreover there was a great piece by Maerten van Heemskerck showing St Luke painting Mary and the child Christ, and a *Last Supper* by the little-known Haarlem artist Master Lucas (died 1562). Add to this Jan de Bray's attractive work *Tending the Orphans* (of 1663) (p. 157), from the Netherlands Reformed Orphanage, and one gets an impression of how much importance the patronage of all the above-mentioned institutions had for the prosperity of the Haarlem School of painters in the sixteenth and seventeenth centuries.

This list should be supplemented with important paintings which used to hang in the town hall and the Princes' Court in Haarlem: a masterly canvas by Hendrick Cornelisz Vroom showing the arrival of the Count Palatine Frederick V at Flushing (in 1613); Cornelis Cornelisz van Haarlem's *Wedding of Peleus and Thetis* (p. 282) (of 1593), as well as Hendrick Pot's heavily symbolic *Apotheosis of Prince William I*; Jan de Bray's *Apotheosis of Frederick Henry* (of 1681) and his *Vulcan and the Cyclops* (of 1683).

All these works were later, in 1862, transferred to Haarlem town hall, where, together with the great paintings by Hals, they came to constitute the Municipal Museum.

The artistic life of Rotterdam was similar to that of Haarlem but on a much more modest scale. Adriaen van der Werff in 1702 painted there an allegory on *Charity*, for a mantelpiece in the House of the Holy Ghost or the Old Men's Home. Another Rotterdam artist made a mantelpiece-painting with *Christ Curing the Lame and Crippled* for the Old Municipal Hospital in the Hoogstraat. The Amsterdam artists achieved little in this field. The three painted panels with governors of the Alms Orphanage engaged on works of charity already mentioned above, by Werner van den Valckert, are rather exceptional for Amsterdam.

Towards the last quarter of the seventeenth century the great period of the Dutch corporation piece ended. The churches and hospitals, too, did not add much to their collections of paintings after that. It is as though the walls of the Doelen halls and the governors' rooms offered no more space; in any event, the houses of private citizens appear from later paintings to be rather full. The painters, when they did not turn to the modern art of decorating ceilings, mantelpieces and walls, mostly went over to the small-size painting. Large canvases became the exception. We have already mentioned one from this period at Haarlem, that by Frans Decker of 1737. In Amsterdam, Cornelis Troost supplied a few governors' portraits during this period, in which he combined the old tradition with the new concepts of lighter colouring and more natural attitudes: in 1724 the inspectors of the College of Medicine; in 1729 his outsize painting of governors of the Almshouse Orphanage; in 1731 his much more modest group of three wardens of the surgeons' guild. As recently as the nineteenth century, Jan Adam Kruseman tried his energies on the governors' group in the now three-hundred-year-old tradition. Only one thing was changed. For the first time the governors and lady governors of the Lepers' House had themselves portrayed together.

The group-portraits of the Civic Guards, the group-portraits of governors of municipal institutions and other paintings from the asylums and hospitals of the great towns in the Republic of the United Netherlands form a unique whole which cannot be equalled anywhere in the world. Compared with this rich source of paintings, which later was to become of the greatest importance to the Dutch museums, the art contribution from local and national government offices has been small. This is because the town halls and government buildings have almost all of them remained in constant use. The mantelpiece-paintings and ceiling-decorations – mostly adorned with biblical, mythological or allegorical scenes – were for the greater part left where they were in the rooms where the magistrates continued working, having meetings and receiving visitors. As a result of a financial agreement in 1804, however, some paintings were transferred from Haarlem town hall to the National Art Gallery, the

19

predecessor of the Rijksmuseum, among them Hendrick Cornelisz Vroom's large canvas of *The Battle on the Lake of Haarlem in 1573*, in which the fleet of the Prince of Orange was defeated by the Spaniards; and another large canvas representing *Adam and Eve in Paradise*, a work by Cornelis Cornelisz of Haarlem (of 1592) which had been given by Haarlem to Prince Maurice to decorate the Court in that town.

In some cases, too, paintings from other local government buildings went to museum collections. Thus a *View of the River IJ* by Hendrick Vroom which now hangs in the Rijksmuseum, came from the Amsterdam Workhouse; while the large panoramic view of the town with the 'Golden Lion' in the foreground (once the flag-ship of Cornelis Tromp), a late masterpiece by Willem van de Velde the Younger, came from the conference-hall of the governors of the Walen (a part of Amsterdam) in the Schreiers Tower.

A set of twelve small pieces, with scenes from the history of the Batavian, Caninefat and Gallic tribes and of the Romans in the Netherlands, by Otto van Veen, alias Vaenius, which the States-General bought as a suitable decoration for the Trèves Hall in the Binnenhof or Houses of Parliament at The Hague (before it got its new decoration), was of no particular interest.

Of more importance to the Dutch museums were to be the paintings decorating the conference-rooms of their Lordships of the Admiralties and the directors of the East Indies, West Indies and Levant Companies. In the Hall of the Seventeen Gentlemen (i. e. the 17 directors of the Dutch East India Company) at Amsterdam could be seen views of the more important Dutch settlements in the Far East and some painted maps. In their conference building at Middelburg one found small portraits of the governors-general of the Dutch East Indies, which were reduced copies of the complete series of lifesize busts which hung in the Castle of Batavia.

The directors of the Levant Company had hanging in their room views of Constantinople, Smyrna and Aleppo. In 1817 this collection was considerably extended through the Calkoen legacy. This contained some dozens of highly striking canvases of receptions at the Court of the Sultan, views of Constantinople and the Bosphorus; paintings

20

of life in the city of the Golden Horn and the surrounding country-side, and of the diverse population to be found there. All this was the work of the Franco-Flemish painter Jean Baptiste Vanmour (1671–1737), who spent his life in Turkey, and of the school he founded there. When these companies were wound up, their property came to the State. Some of the paintings they owned unfortunately went astray; the remainder were added to the nation's museum collections. There these pictures give a vivid impression of early Dutch commerce and shipping in distant lands. Sometimes they are of a especially good quality, for instance a large canvas by Hendrick Cornelisz Vroom (p. 298) on which the Amsterdam four-master – the only one the city possessed in the seventeenth century – is depicted on the river IJ on the occasion of its return from Brazil. The canvas belonged to the West India Company.

Like the works of art and historic relics from the conference-halls of the trading companies, those belonging to the Admiralties (the Republic had five of them) came after the latter had been disbanded to the State. The Rijksmuseum was only enriched by a few paintings, but among them were important pieces such as the great ceremonial portrait of *Michiel Adriaenszoon de Ruyter* (p. 292) by Ferdinand Bol, of 1667, which the Admiral himself had donated to the Admiralty of Middelburg where he had formerly served; a canvas by Johannes Lingelbach showing the *Battle of Leghorn* in 1652, and rare views of Algiers, Tunis, Tangier and Syracuse by Reinier Nooms called Zeeman.

It is hardly possible to overestimate the significance of all these works of art for the Dutch museums. But for them an institution like the Rijksmuseum would lack its highlights and the Frans Hals Museum in Haarlem would probably not have existed at all. How these paintings eventually found their way there will be shown in a subsequent chapter.

FAMILY PORTRAITS

From the fifteenth century onwards the Princes of the country had their portraits painted, but the revolt against Philip II resulted in no personal property of the Hapsburg-Burgundian house being left in Holland or Zeeland. What had not been damaged by fire or the adversities of the time was sent to Madrid or Vienna. From the possessions of the other powerful House reigning in the east of the country, the Dukes of Gelderland, nothing in the way of paintings or art objects has been left either. We cannot even estimate approximately what there must have been[1]. The possessions of the bishops of Utrecht fared no better, apart from a few paraments.

However, history in this period is not concerned only with the princes of the country but also with the high nobility, whose position and wealth had increased enormously in the course of the fifteenth century. These noblemen lived almost like princes; they were related to the most important German ruling families, to the sovereigns of France and Lorraine, to the Burgundians or even the Hapsburgs. Following the example given by the princes, they too formed collections of family portraits in their castles or in their palaces at Brussels.

In this field we have most accurate information about the family of Nassau. It is true that we have no details going back to the fifteenth or the first half of the sixteenth centuries but inventory-lists of the Nassau palaces from subsequent generations supply the information which is lacking from earlier days. In 1632, for example, a portrait of Henry III of Nassau-Breda, a great-uncle of the Prince of Orange, was to be seen in the quarters of the Stadtholder in the Binnenhof at The Hague. Unfortunately the inventory does not mention by whose hand it was painted, and so we can only guess that it may have been one of the portraits which Jan Gossaert made of the Count. In the same year there hung in the 'Old Court', the palace in the Noord-einde at The Hague, portraits of René of Orange-Chalon (the cousin who was killed in battle in 1544 and from whom Prince William I

---

[1] The portrait of Duke Charles of Gelder in the Municipal Museum of Arnhem is an inferior copy of later date and does not originate from ducal possessions.

received the rich inheritance of Orange, Breda and many other territories in the Netherlands) and of his wife Anna of Lorraine, paintings, therefore, of the fourth decade of the sixteenth century which must have been transferred from Brussels or Breda to The Hague, unless they were copies. In the Court of Nassau at Brussels there were also family portraits. In 1618 mention is made of one of Count Engelbert II of Nassau-Breda (1451–1504). It has been suggested that this was perhaps identical with the small panel by the so-called 'Master of the royal portraits' which in 1933 entered the Rijksmuseum as a donation of Dr H. W. C. Tietje of Amsterdam. In the time of Prince William I (1533–1584) several paintings were added to the Nassau Collection. In the first place there were the portraits of Prince William I himself with his first wife, Anna van Buren, by Antonio Moro, of 1555. Later they were the property of his youngest son, Frederick Henry, but afterwards they disappeared without trace. However, we can obtain an idea of the lost pieces from a replica of the portrait of the prince in the Cassel Museum, and a copy (of lesser quality) of that of the princess in the Palace of Mantua. At a later age the 'Father of the Fatherland' was painted by Adriaen Key (p. 16), among others.

After the death of Prince William, the Nassaus continued to commission portraits and before long they had large collections. After the worst distress of the early years of the Eighty Years War against Spain was over, court life in The Hague began to flourish. To decorate his palace in the Binnenhof, where the military element predominated, Prince Maurice ordered from Jan Anthonisz Ravestein portraits of his leading officers. This commission grew into a series of over twenty canvases which today belong to the Mauritshuis. In the same period small portraits were made of members of the House of Nassau and generals in Dutch service, a collection which later, during the Stadtholdership of Frederick Henry, was extended. Prince Maurice himself was painted by Michiel Miereveld (p. 293). This large panel, in which the Stadtholder was portrayed standing, in his gilded state armour, the badge of the Order of the Garter on a blue ribbon round his neck, is a monumental piece worthy of the great prince.

The Nassau portrait-collection was further extended during the Stadtholdership of Frederick Henry (1625–1647). Gerard Honthorst painted the Prince, the Princess, their four daughters and their son, William II. In the making of replicas, for which there was a constant demand, the artist was assisted by his brother Willem and probably by others. Ravestein and Miereveld also continued working for the Stadtholder. The Princess, Amalia of Solms, moreover commissioned portraits of her sisters.

Other Nassaus soon followed this example. The cousins living in Leeuwarden, in particular, commissioned the Friesian painter Wybrand de Geest (by marriage a brother-in-law of Rembrandt). When in 1641 the youthful William II of Orange married the eldest daughter of Charles I of England–the first royal marriage in the House of Nassau!–Anthony van Dyck painted the wedding-portrait (p. 280), his last work which he was not even able to complete. A few years later, in 1652, Princess Mary, as a young widow, posed before Bartholomeus van der Helst (p. 294). Another portrait of her, in which she appeared attired in a Brazilian feather-coat, was made by Adriaen Hannemann (not Jan Mijtens, as used to be assumed).

A generation later Caspar Netscher, Godfried Schalcken and Willem Wissing (after an example set by Sir Peter Lely) painted portraits of William III and Princess Mary Stuart.

In the eighteenth century William IV was painted by Frans van der Mijn, the Frenchman Jacques André Joseph Aved and the Swede Hans Hysing, while his wife, the Princess Royal, Anna of Hanover, commissioned Johann Heinrich Tischbein to paint her portrait. Under their son William V, court life in The Hague flourished as never before. A number of artists were now commissioned to paint the Stadtholder and his wife, their three children, and later also their son- and daughter-in-law. In this connection mention must be made of a series of fine pastels by J. F. A. Tischbein (p. 304) and also of works by T. P. C. Haag, J. G. Ziesenis, B. S. Bolomey and several other artists, as well as a large number of miniatures. King William I, after the French period, handed over all these paintings to the Rijksmuseum and the Mauritshuis. They form part of the core of these institutions.

The commissions given by the Nassaus to portrait-painters did not stand alone. In the years when Moro painted Prince William I and

Anna van Buren, he also worked for the Count and Countess of Egmond, the Hoornes, the Marquis and Marchioness of Bergen-op-Zoom and many other members of the high nobility. It is an inestimable loss that from all this work no originals remain. Much of the old portrait-collections of nobles must, in the sixteenth century, have gone to the Southern Netherlands, for it was there, at and round the Court, that almost all great families moved.

But in the meantime another class arose in the Northern Netherlands which stood ready to take the place of the aristocracy, the rich bourgeoisie of the trading cities. In comparison, the role played by the lesser nobility in the Northern Netherlands in the history of the portrait has only been small. In the second quarter of the sixteenth century Dutch merchants started commissioning portraits. We think, for instance, of the paintings of the Treasurer and Alderman of Amsterdam, *Pieter Bicker* (1495–1567) and his charming wife, *Anna Codde* (p. 113), by Maerten van Heemskerck, of 1529. From the same period comes the captivating portrait by Dirck Jacobsz of *Pompejus Occo* (p. 119), the commercial magnate, who has sometimes been called the first 'mercator sapiens' of Amsterdam. Thereafter the well-to-do citizens of the Dutch towns, of Amsterdam and Haarlem, Utrecht, Middelburg and Dordrecht, The Hague, Delft, Zierikzee and several others, added to their collections of family portraits from one generation to the next in the same way as did the House of Orange-Nassau.

Many of these paintings later found their way into museums, almost invariably as legacies from childless people, the last of their generation or branch of their family. The first such legacy was received by the Rijksmuseum in 1823: twenty-two portraits from Mrs Balguerie née van Rijswijk. Both important and characteristic of Dutch art was the collection of fifty-two paintings, mainly family portraits, bequeathed to the museum in 1880 by Jonkheer J. S. H. van de Poll, descendant and heir of several Amsterdam governing families. This collection contained, among others, the famous painting of *Elisabeth Bas* (p. 292) by Ferdinand Bol (earlier, but wrongly, attributed to Rembrandt), his paintings of her grandchildren, the Meulenaer couple (p. 292), the portrait of *Pieter Schout* (p. 175) on horseback, a real gem by Thomas de Keyser, panels by Nicolaes Elias and several other artists.

Another typical Amsterdam legacy was that of the Dowager Jonkheer J. J. van Winter, née Bicker. In 1880 she bequeathed forty-four family portraits to the city which in 1885 were transferred to the Rijksmuseum. In 1884 Jonkheer J. H. F. K. van Swinderen gave twenty-six family portraits to the Rijksmuseum, among them those of *Jan van Riebeeck*, the founder of Capetown, and his wife (of 1650), good works by the hand of Dirck Craey, who is still too little appreciated. Particularly important were thirty-five portraits of members of Amsterdam and Haarlem ruling families, which Jonkheer J. S. R. van de Poll of Arnhem donated in 1885 to the Rijksmuseum, with works by Frans Hals and Bartholomeus van der Helst among them.

An excellent example of a Zeeland family collection was the twenty-five portraits bequeathed in 1876 by Jonkheer Jacob de Witte van Citters to the Netherlands Museum at The Hague. In 1885 they were transferred to the Rijksmuseum. Since then, nowhere can the attractive work of Salomon Mesdach of Middelburg be studied so well as in Amsterdam. The De Witte van Citters legacy included no fewer than six of his works, dating from the years 1619–1625 (p. 131). A very fine pair of portraits left by P. de Clercq and P. van Eeghen and their wives was offered to the city of Amsterdam in 1891: the portraits of *Lucas de Clercq* (p. 284) and *Feyntje van Steenkiste,* painted in 1635 by Frans Hals, and among his best works. Amsterdam added these canvases to the large number of paintings on loan to the Rijksmuseum. In 1903/1910 Jonkheer Salomon Rendrop bequeathed to the Rijksmuseum the fine portraits of the Amsterdam alderman *François de Vicq* and his wife *Aletta Pancras* (p. 295), by Gerard ter Borch; in 1902 J. M. Willink van Bennebroeck donated *The Family Group of David Leeuw* by Abraham van den Tempel, as well as some forty other paintings. Finally there was the impressive loan of 1897 by the Van Weede family which included the portrait of the young *Maria Trip* (p. 290) by Rembrandt, a portrait which had never left the hands of her descendants, and Casper Netscher's painting of *Lady Philippa Staunton,* wife of Roelof van Arkel, Lord of Burgst (of 1668).

This list, though long, is still not complete. It gives an impression of how a large number of portraits from many of the most prominent Dutch families, in particular from Amsterdam, came together in the Rijksmuseum. But for these donations the great Dutch portrait-painters such as Rembrandt, Ferdinand Bol, Frans Hals, Ter Borch and so many others, would only have been poorly represented in the Rijksmuseum.

Moreover the museum increased its collections by purchases of family possessions. In this manner, for instance, the monumental group of the *Family of Rutger Jan Schimmelpenninck* (p. 267) by Pierre Paul Prud'hon (Drucker-Fraser bequest) became museum property in 1929; and in 1950 so did the pastels of the Van der Waeyen couple by Jan Baptiste Perronneau. When the State of the Netherlands bought the highly important collection of Michiel Adriaenszoon de Ruyter and his descendants for the Rijksmuseum in 1896, it included numerous portraits of the great Admiral, his family and issue (p. 292).

From other Dutch museums, too, one can realise how important are the family portraits, to which each generation added and which were carefully preserved. In 1883 the museum in Haarlem acquired through inheritance the family collection of Jonkheer Johan Carel Willem Fabricius van Leyenburg. It constituted a unique acquisition, comprising the portraits of his ancestors from nearly all periods of the Haarlem school, and a number of non-Haarlem masters, from the beginning of the seventeenth century up to Jan Adam Kruseman, and the fashionable French painter Alexandre Jean Dubois Drahouet of the early nineteenth century. By far the most impressive pieces were, of course, the portraits of the Haarlem burgomaster Nicolaes van de Meer and his wife Cornelia Vooght Claesdochter by Frans Hals. Immediately after these in quality came the paintings of the Colen-bergh couple by Johannes Verspronck, a small group of the Colen-bergh van Braeckel family by Gerard ter Borch, a good work by Miereveld and four decorative paintings by Nicolaes Maes. Further-more, the collection included works of seventeenth-century masters such as Dirck Hals, Johannes Victor, Pieter Nason, Daniël Haringh,

Jan Weenix and Theodorus Netscher, works of the eighteenth-century painters Frans Decker, B. S. Bolomey and J. M. Quinkhard, two charming children's heads by Tako Jelgersma and, finally, a canvas by Charles Howard Hodges.

In 1888 Miss F. A. C. van der Burch bequeathed to the museum a number of family portraits, including works by J. A. van Ravesteyn, Jan de Bray, Constantijn Netscher, Johannes Verkolje and various anonymous painters.

In the next year the museum was enriched by a donation from J. T. Gerlings, among which was an elaborate example of Michiel Miereveld's abilities: the portrait of Gilles de Clarges, once again a good set of portraits by Verspronck and, furthermore, paintings by Caspar Netscher, Jean Henri Brandon, Wybrandt de Geest, Johannes van Haensbergen and François Verwilt. It is thanks to all these gifts and legacies that the Haarlem museum can show the public a fairly complete survey of the important local school.

The Mauritshuis, small in size and more national than local in character, has acquired fewer family portraits. Only some donations in this particular field are worth mentioning. Thus, in 1904, a portrait of a doctor of the Van Hogendorp family, painted by Thomas de Keyser in 1636, was bequeathed by the Dowager A. L. T. A. Grisart, née Baroness van Hogendorp van Hofwegen. The largest legacy of family portraits which the Mauritshuis acquired was the collection left in 1907 by Maria Johanna Singendonck. It consisted mainly of late seventeenth- and eighteenth-century paintings.

That the family portrait was of small importance for the Rotterdam museum, can be explained partly by the history of the town. In the time of the Republic, Rotterdam was not among the large towns of Holland. Although trade and shipping flourished, it never had the patrician population of the 'old' towns, and the art of portraiture did not flourish particularly. So the paintings which the town possessed did not, for the greater part, find their way into the Boymans Museum but into the History Museum of Rotterdam, as their historic value is greater than their aesthetic significance.

CABINETS OF PAINTINGS

The official name of the Mauritshuis is the Royal Cabinet of Paintings. This somewhat old-fashioned title indicates that the museum is neither a collection of portraits from public institutions, gathered over the years, nor one of family portraits, but that it grew from a cabinet of paintings. Although the Mauritshuis also contains portraits from the House of Orange and elsewhere, in comparison with the 'cabinet pieces' these are of minor importance.

Cabinets of paintings already existed in the Netherlands at the end of the sixteenth century. Carel van Mander mentions quite a number of them in his *Book of Painters* which was published in 1604 in Haarlem. Much of the knowledge he possessed of the art of his own and earlier times he owed to the owners of these collections who had kindly shown him their treasures. Thus he writes about the triptych of the *Dance round the Golden Calf* (pp. 104–5), a masterpiece by Lucas van Leyden which he admired somewhere in Amsterdam in the house of a private collector whose name he regrettably does not mention. In the house of Dirck van Sonnevelt, Van Mander saw a second work by Lucas executed in water-colour, while he found a third piece by the same master at the house of one Knotter who himself painted. Another collector in whose cabinet Van Mander could see many paintings, was Jacques Razet of Amsterdam, a public notary, many-sided humanist, poet, collector, painter and great friend of the arts. He also possessed works by Van Mander himself. A whole series of Amsterdamers – the majority of them merchants – were collecting paintings at this time.

In other towns of Holland and Zeeland – in Haarlem, Leyden, Delft and Middelburg – one also found cabinets of paintings in those days. Some of them must have been truly magnificent. The merchant and painter Jacob Engbrechtsz Rauwert (died 1597), for instance, who was collecting as early as 1546, probably owned Albert van Ouwater's *Resurrection of Lazarus,* the masterpiece of Northern-Netherlandish painting of the Middle Ages, which in 1573 was stolen by the Spanish soldiers and is now in Berlin. Moreover he owned fine panels by Brueghel and Pieter Aertsz.

Of all these private collections, we unfortunately know little more than the mere names of the owners and the titles of the works they possessed. Later their collections were broken up, without the date and the particular circumstances under which this happened being known to us. But the most important thing was that the taste for collecting continued. The generation that came after Van Mander's bought what the previous generation sold. One cabinet of paintings followed another; selling stimulated buying. A tradition was thereby established and flourished widely.

The collecting of paintings became a hobby of the well-to-do population in the rich trading towns. The nobility hardly took part in this at all. If a nobleman later occasionally formed a cabinet of paintings, this was for a town house, which then differed neither in itself nor in its use from a bourgeois house.

Finally the princes of Europe, too, began to set up cabinets of paintings. Following the example of the Dutch bourgeoisie, they collected, besides the great Italian masters and those of the Antwerp school, the lovely but typically bourgeois art of the Northern-Netherlandish school. Thus works by Potter, Steen and Rembrandt and the landscapes with shepherds and cattle of the Italianisers, canvases and panels by Wouwermans, Dou, Van Mieris and many others, found their way abroad to the palaces of German princes at Brunswick, Cassel, Düsseldorf, Berlin and Dresden; to the country residences of eager English lords; even to the Florence of Cosimo III de Medici, the Paris of Louis XIV, and the Regent of Orleans, and distant St Petersburg, where Catherine the Great bought Dutch paintings on a very large scale.

As a result of all this a lively trade in paintings arose, with Amsterdam as its centre. The international importance of this town is shown by the fact that a well-known Parisian like Gersaint came to Holland to get to know the principles applied in auctioneering.

The Wardens of the Guild of St Luke at Haarlem, 1675,
by Jan de Bray (1627–1697) and others.
Canvas. 130×184 cm. (51¹/₈″ ×72¹/₂″). Rijksmuseum No. 614.

It was mainly at the great sales in the former Herenlogement (Hotel for Gentlemen) in Amsterdam (it stood in the place now occupied by the Binnengasthuis, one of the city's large hospitals), that Prince Eugene of Savoy gathered the precious collection of paintings now hanging in Turin, when he spent the winter in Amsterdam, between the campaigns against the French army in the Southern Netherlands. The abundance of good paintings was such that Holland was able to afford these 'blood-lettings', without itself being seriously impoverished. The lack of great, really monumental landscapes by Aelbert Cuyp in the Dutch Museums forms a regrettable exception to this general rule.

One irreparable effect of this lively art trade in the eighteenth century, however, was that all canvases by prominent Italian masters who, as we know, were represented in great numbers and beauty in Holland in the middle of the seventeenth century, left the country. There was Raphael's famous portrait of *Count Castiglione*, for example, of which Rembrandt made a sketch when it was auctioned in Amsterdam in 1639 after coming from the estate of the late Antwerp banker Lucas van Uffelen (drawing in the Albertina in Vienna). The buyer of the painting was Alfonso Lopez, a great Jewish dealer of Spanish descent, through whose hands went many paintings, including the *Flora* by Titian (Uffizi, Florence) and his so-called *Ariosto* (National Gallery, London). Lopez sold the portrait of Castiglione to Mazarin, as a result of which it later came to the Louvre.

Apart from this the Tuscan, Roman and Umbrian schools were not particularly popular in the Northern Netherlands. At that time the great Venetians of the sixteenth century were the best liked. Dutchmen did not favour the trecento or the quattrocento, with the exception of Mantegna and Giovanni Bellini. They were, however, interested in the works of Baroccio, Domenichino and especially of the Bolognese group, the Carracci, Guercino and Guido Reni; and later in the eighteenth century, artists like Albani, Castiglione, Carlo Maratti and Trevisani were appreciated. This taste was not merely Dutch for everywhere in Europe connoisseurs praised this kind of painting.

The best known collector of Italian art of the seventeenth century was Gerrit Reynst. After his death the most important part of his cabinet, twenty-four paintings and twelve statues, was shipped in 1660 to England as a present from the States-General to King Charles II who had just succeeded to the throne. On this they were willing to spend no less than Fls. 80,000 (today the 'Dutch gift' is one of the sights of Hampton Court). Many Dutchmen able to afford it were trying in the seventeenth century to follow the examples of Van Uffelen, Lopez and Reynst.

Compared with Italian masterpieces, considered so desirable by the great collectors, Dutch paintings in this period were less interesting to the experts, and they were therefore quite cheap. But just because of their cheapness, they were within the reach of many and this may explain the large number of collections in the seventeenth century.

In the eighteenth century the situation changed. The expensive Italian pictures had by then already left the country, not because Holland held a sale from a bankrupt estate, as it were, but because of a change in taste. Just as in the new century the so-called 'minor' Dutch and Flemish masters became more and more in demand in Paris and elsewhere abroad for their intimacy and their cosy atmosphere, no less than for their incredibly high artistic qualities while the new fashionable small rooms with their panelling and silk-hung wall sections no longer offered space for the monumental Italian pieces executed 'in the grand style'. So these artists were also reappraised in their own country. At the auctions the fiercely covered pearls of Dutch painting began to form the highlights of many collectors' cabinets and the general competition at home and abroad raised their prices to new heights.

It is impossible to describe here the whole history of the cabinet of paintings in the Netherlands. I restrict myself therefore, by way of example, to mentioning the famous collections of Pieter van der Lip (auctioned in Amsterdam in 1712), Gerrit Braamcamp of Amsterdam (auctioned in 1771) and Joachim Rendorp (Amsterdam auction on 1st October 1793), at which *The Pantry* (p. 239) of Pieter de Hooch, his *Mother's Duties* and his *Linen Cupboard* (p. 296) – three major works now belonging to the Rijksmuseum – came respectively under the hammer. In the Van der Lip Cabinet probably also hung Vermeer's *Woman in Blue, Reading a Letter* (p. 296). Gerrit Braamcamp possessed, furthermore, Jan Steen's *Merry Homecoming, The Fish Vendor* (p. 229) by Adriaen van Ostade and Rembrandt's little portrait of Dr Ephraim Bueno (all three of them now in the Rijksmuseum). Thus one found in many Dutch cabinets works which are now world-famous.

It has been the fate of these collections that, generally speaking, they were quite soon broken up. The merchant-class in the Netherlands had no long-standing traditions. The eighteenth-century collections that stayed together only did so because, at a fortunate moment, they had been included in their entirety in what later became public museums. It is these collections which in particular deserve our attention.

First of all the Cabinet of Paintings of the Stadtholders. Its founder was Johan Willem Friso. Whether in this he was following the example of the rich Dutch merchants or that of his princely German relatives, such as the Landgraves of Hessen-Kassel, cannot be established. On the backs of his paintings the Prince had his collection marks put, and these can still be found on several works now hanging in the Mauritshuis. His early death in 1711 caused a lengthy standstill in the extension of the collection, but his posthumously born son, Willem Carel Hendrik Friso, later the Stadtholder William IV, continued it after reaching manhood. He did this together with his wife, the English Princess Royal, Anna of Hanover, who herself painted.

When he had become Stadtholder of all Dutch provinces in 1747 and had established himself in The Hague, the Prince was able to indulge his love for the arts more liberally. The most important purchase he made was in 1749, when the painter Frans Decker, at the auction of Willem Fabricius at Haarlem acquired for the Stadtholder the large canvas of *The Young Bull* (p. 299) by Potter at the price of Fls. 630. The painting was not expensive; a *Flight to Egypt* by Adriaen van der Werff, purchased shortly before, had cost Fls. 2,500. *The Young Bull* received a place among the earlier purchases for the cabinet of the Prince and, since then, has always been a most popular work of art–because of the incredible realism with which the cattle, the bird in the air and the frog in the foreground have been painted

35

and, not least, because of the unusually large size of this remarkable canvas.

It was not given to William IV to devote himself for long to his hobby. When he died in 1751 he was only forty years old; his son and heir, William V, was then only three. In due course, however, he too extended the collection he had inherited from his father. In this, as in everything else he undertook, he received the support of his guardian, Duke Ernst Ludwig von Brunswick-Wolfenbüttel. This Prince of Orange, who was very wealthy, spent large sums on purchases of good paintings. Partly on the advice of the painter T. P. C. Haag, who from 1752 had been keeper of the Stadtholder's collection, he made purchases at the auction of the cabinet of the late Willem Lornier, which was held at The Hague in 1763. Many paintings from this sale, however, which contained no fewer than 353 items, went to the cabinet of A. L. van Heteren to which we shall refer later. In this collection there were famous canvases such as the *Feast of St Nicolas* (p. 289) and *The Parrot's Cage* (p. 237) by Jan Steen. A year later, at the sale of the cabinet of the late Benjamin da Costa in the Hague, once again purchases were made on behalf of the Prince. In 1765 he bought four paintings at the Pieter Leendert de Neufville sale at Amsterdam and another six from the collection of the Elector of Saxony, also auctioned there. In 1766 another six were bought at the sale of paintings belonging to Catharina de la Court, née Backer, inherited from Mr de la Court van der Voort, and his son. The Prince also acquired pieces from the art dealer Pieter IJver (Amsterdam, 1769) and Gerrit Braamcamp (Amsterdam, 1771).

But the largest increase in the Stadtholder's collection was the purchase in 1768 of the entire Van Slingelandt cabinet, the best the Netherlands had to offer at that time. For many years the owner, Govert van Slingelandt, Lord of the Lindt, Chief Tax Collector for the Province of Holland and West Friesland (1694–1767), had aimed specifically at increasing the artistic quality of his cabinet. He had voluntarily imposed on himself the restriction that his cabinet should not exceed forty pieces. Whenever a painting of exceptionally fine quality came on the market he tried to acquire it, but then disposed of a lesser piece. Sometimes he was forced to buy up entire collections in order to obtain a single item. What did not interest him went back to auction.

In his will Van Slingelandt had laid down that after his death his collection was to be auctioned. But the Stadtholder, who knew the reputation of the cabinet, approached the heirs with the request that he be allowed to buy it privately as it stood. They refused on the strength of the provisions of the will. William V was indeed not the only applicant. The French Minister of Foreign Affairs, too, the Duc de Choiseul, who himself was an important collector, made enquiries from the heirs. Perhaps his attention had been drawn to it by the 'directeur-général des batiments, jardins, arts et manufactures du roi', the Marquis de Marigny, who with his travelling companion, the engraver Cochin, had visited Van Slingelandt's cabinet in 1767, when he accorded it high praise. The French Diplomatic Agent at The Hague, Desrivaux, made great efforts on behalf of his master in Paris. The Empress of Russia, Catherine II, also asked for information regarding the collection. But William V insisted, indicating his willingness to spend a very large amount on the paintings and at last the heirs succumbed to the then enormous sum of Fls. 50,000, the Prince having finally left it open to them to decide themselves what price they would accept.

As a result of this wonderful acquisition the Stadtholder's cabinet became the richest ever known in the Netherlands. Apart from a choice selection of Dutch painting from the seventeenth century, it included excellent Flemish works from the same period and, furthermore, works by Italians, some French pieces and four sublime Holbeins which had come from William III. Neither the holding of family portraits of earlier date and other items like the fine miniatures from the palaces in Friesland, as well as works of art from the Castle of Oranienstein near Dietz in Nassau, nor later legacies, purchases and donations, however important, could change the character of the Prince's cabinet afterwards. Generally speaking, history has not been very grateful to William V for what he did as Stadtholder but this judgement does not apply to his praiseworthy activity as a collector. For to him – even more than to his father and grandfather – we owe the unrivalled quality of the Mauritshuis collection.

The cabinets of paintings existing at the time of the Republic of the United Netherlands have been of less significance in the formation of what was eventually to become the Rijksmuseum. Admittedly, in this instance too, famous cabinets were included which considerably increased the quality of the museum's collections but, being among such numerous paintings of different origin, they never came to dominate the museum. The most important cabinets to enter the Rijksmuseum, those of Gerrit van der Pot van Groeneveld of Rotterdam and of A. L. van Heteren, will be discused later.

The history of the Haarlem Museum was not affected by cabinets of paintings. The Rotterdam museum was to a certain extent, but in a manner all its own, as we shall see in a later chapter.

We do not wish to conclude this chapter without recalling, as an illustration of the spirit which imbued the eighteenth century collector, an interesting and many-sided Amsterdam citizen of the time, Cornelis Ploos van Amstel (1726–1798). In the first place this timber-broker was important as a collector of paintings, drawings and prints, of Rembrandt among others. But he did not stop there. Even before this time some collectors, proud of their art treasures, had had prints made of them. Ploos aimed at the same thing and undertook the work himself, to which end he invented a new technique which he was able to apply most successfully, in particular for the reproduction of drawings in pencil, chalk and watercolour. In 1765 he described his invention in a book. This many-sided man also wrote about the theory of the fine arts and on anatomy for artists. Moreover he manipulated pencil and brush. He stood in the centre of the artistic life of the Amsterdam of his time, associated with artists like Isaäc de Moucheron, Jacob de Wit, Jacobus Buys and Cornelis Troost, whose daughter he married. Thus his significance and that of his collection went much beyond that of a mere collector for pleasure. The spread of knowledge of the art of Dutch painting and drawing owes much to the work of such men.

THE FIRST DUTCH MUSEUM

Museums in Western Europe owe their existence to the French Revolution. But just as that did not break out completely without warning, so the museums, too, had their period of preparation. During the Age of Enlightenment it had been suggested that the large collections of prominent gentlemen, who usually allowed them to be viewed by those interested, should be opened to the general public. Florence and Rome led the way in this, France followed. In 1750, 110 paintings belonging to the King were exhibited in the Palais du Luxembourg; together with the large Rubens Gallery they could be viewed twice a week. This was Europe's first public museum of paintings. It did not exist for long because Louis XVI soon wanted to have the palace put at his disposal again to accommodate his elder brother. In the end however, in 1793 – that is, after the fall of the Bourbons – the Louvre was opened as a large museum of paintings. Before long it was to be immeasurably enriched by the enormous number of art-treasures which Italy and other countries were forced to surrender to France as war tribute. Thus the Louvre (named Musée Napoléon during the Empire) soon became the radiant centre towards which the eyes of every art-lover were automatically drawn. As with so many things in that period, the achievements of Paris stimulated others to emulation.

The Netherlands were late to follow this lead. When the old Republic was 'liberated' in 1795 by the French Army, one of the first acts of the 'liberators' was to pack the cabinet of paintings of the Stadtholder William V, who had fled to England, and to send it to Paris. This was merely a repetition of what the victorious generals of the Directoire had, in the past years, done so often in Italy. Nobody protested. On the following 28th September the 'Batavians' sold part of the Prince's furniture in the Buitenhof at The Hague. A second auction of his furniture was held in the Huis ten Bosch, a palace near The Hague on 16th August 1797. This time paintings had been added as well, but not the family portraits; a third sale took place on 23rd July 1798; a fourth and fifth followed later that year.

But in the meantime a change had taken place which turned out to be of great significance: on 26th July 1798 the College of Administration of the Property of the former Stadtholder was dismissed; henceforth all letters regarding the domains had to be addressed to the Agent of Finance, Izaak Jan Alexander Gogel. It was he who, acting on a suggestion made in the National Assembly by Albert Jan Verbeek (a man interested in the past), made a museum from what remained of the art-treasures from the Orange Palaces. No doubt Gogel, who, as a patriot, was pro-French, was guided by the example of Paris.

He approached the task energetically and without delay. By 3rd August 1798 he was already writing to 'citizen' Vermeulen at Leeuwarden, asking him not to sell the paintings in the Nassau Palaces in Friesland but to ship them to The Hague. These instructions were not carried out but he succeeded a little later in getting the paintings from the palace of Het Loo to The Hague. For the time being they were stored with the rest of the Oranges family portraits in the Huis ten Bosch. On 12th January 1799 the art-dealer Cornelis Sebille Roos (1754–1820) was appointed to supervise them.

In his town of birth Amsterdam, Roos had already had some experience in this field, for in 1798 he had been the first to organise a permanent art gallery, in the northern wing of the Trippenhuis. He received the title of Inspector of the Art Gallery of the Huis ten Bosch; it was stipulated that he had to make an inventory of the paintings and to exhibit them. No sooner had Roos received his appointment than he set about finding out whether any paintings were to be found elsewhere which would qualify for the art gallery. In the palace of Soestdijk he found good canvases by Lairesse, Glauber and Melchior d'Hondecoeter which were promptly sent to The Hague. At the beginning of 1799 paintings from the Admiralty of Amsterdam were added to them, among which was a portrait of *Michiel de Ruyter* (p. 292) by Ferdinand Bol. Next, canvases and panels from the government buildings at the Binnenhof entered the Huis ten Bosch, and then some from the Maritime Office at Rotterdam.

With due speed all these paintings were arranged in the Huis ten Bosch to make a presentable whole so that, on 31st May 1800, the doors of the National Art Gallery could be opened to everybody who considered a visit to the first public museum in the Netherlands worth sixpence (later the price of admission rose to elevenpence even).

Less than two weeks later the first purchase was announced: the large painting of *The Threatened Swan* (p. 173) by Jan Asselijn. Now followed a long series of purchases by which, in varying degree, the two aims underlying the foundation of the museum were observed. On the one hand it sought after artistically valuable pieces to replace the Stadtholder's Cabinet seized by the French; on the other hand efforts were made to obtain works depicting the country's past. A sharp distinction between the two does not appear to have been made. It is remarkable but understandable, in view of these basic aims, that nobody thought of buying works by foreigners. Thus a Potter, Wijnands, Teniers, Wouwerman, Ruysdael and a Rembrandt, which later turned out to be a work by Fabritius, were bought, together with a portrait of Oldenbarneveldt by Moreelse, the seabattle off Leghorn by Reinier Nooms, and Bartholomeus van der Helst's portraits of the Admiral Aert van Nes and his wife. Together with such paintings there were also portraits of the heroes of their own time, in particular of the Fourth English Sea War. The painter Cornelis van Cuylenburg (1758–1827) painted them in 1801: the one of the Rear-Admiral Willem Crul (who was killed in battle in 1781 and who had been an uncle of Gogel's) he copied from an original by J. J. Heinsius; of the Vice-Admiral Arnold Jan Zoutman, who died in 1793, he made a posthumous portrait. The museum had now become fairly up-to-date. When the flow of visitors became satisfactory, the painter Jan Gerard Waldorp was appointed as expert to show the public round the museum. In 1801 the first, admittedly very short, catalogue (by Waldorp) appeared.

In the meantime Gogel remained interested in the development of the museum. He even donated a sum from his own pocket for making purchases. In this period of change and financial ruin it was not difficult to acquire good paintings in the Netherlands. Roos made extensive use of the opportunity. There were also donations; for example, in 1803 J. Zoutman gave the portraits of his parents. The acquisitions of 1804 were important, for it was then that the town of Haarlem, in an exchange transaction, handed over the paintings already discussed in our second chapter.

The museum in the Huis ten Bosch did not remain in existence for long. It was closed in May 1805 when the Grand-Pensionary, Rutger Jan Schimmelpenninck wanted the building as his summer residence. The paintings now had to be moved. They found accommodation in the building at the corner of the Buitenhof which had formerly held the Stadtholder's cabinet. Thus the tradition of his private collection was now, in a different form, continued by the State.

The history of the National Art Gallery ends with the advent of Louis Napoleon as King of Holland. By a decree of 20th November, 1806, the first year of his reign, this monarch, inspired by the best intentions for his new kingdom, appointed a commission with the task of enquiring what institutions existed in France for science and the fine arts, the aim being to promote similar institutions in the Kingdom of Holland. By the same decree the post of Director-General of Arts and Sciences was created, to which Johan Meerman, Lord of Vuren and Dalem (1753–1815) was appointed in 1807. Attention now became concentrated even more than before on museums as such and the way in which they had been organised and liberally enriched in France through the revolution. It suited Louis Napoleon, who had a taste for the fine arts, to emulate the Paris Musée Napoléon in his own kingdom. It was now 1808 and the King had conceived the plan of moving his residence to Amsterdam. He wished to make this city into a centre of arts and sciences for the further glory of his Kingdom. On his arrival he settled in the only building sufficiently large and dignified to serve as a palace, the seventeenth-century town hall at the Dam. The municipal government had to leave it hastily, but part of the municipal art collection remained in the large and small Court-Martial Chambers. The collection could remain there without difficulty, for the Court did not need these rooms. In any case nobody knew what to do with the excessively large paintings. The King therefore moved in, to join *The Nightwatch* and its companions.

On the first day after his arrival in Amsterdam, on 21st April 1808, the King ordered the erection of a great Royal Museum. For the time being it would be housed in some upper rooms at the palace. The active force behind all this was Meerman. To him, probably more even than to the King, we owe the Rijksmuseum.

Louis Napoleon's liberality towards his new creation enabled Meerman to make some very important purchases before long. On 6th June 1808 a choice cabinet of paintings which had been collected by Gerrit van der Pot van Groeneveld was sold at Rotterdam. The Royal Museum was enabled to buy works from it a price of more than one hundred thousand guilders, an unheard-of sum in those days. This was an acquisition on a grand scale comprising, in particular, paintings by seventeenth-century Dutch masters, works by Dou, Van Beyeren, Both, De Witte, Ruysdael, Van der Helst, Potter, Willem van de Velde, Wouwerman, etc. A painting attributed to Van Eyck – *A Gothic Temple with Figures* – was a curious 'odd man out'. It was in fact *The Holy Family and their Kindred* by Geertgen tot Sint Jans. For the time being everything was transferred to The Hague but in July the King ordered that the purchases, together with the contents of the erstwhile National – now Royal – Art Gallery, should be sent to the palace in Amsterdam.

Rich and varied as this collection now was, it was still without anything by Rembrandt. The city of Amsterdam filled the gap, however, by transferring seven large canvases, two of them Rembrandts, to the museum on 15th August 1808, and from then on these were its highlights: *The Nightwatch* (pp. 184–185), and *The Governors of the Cloth-Guild* (p. 197), *The Banquet of the Civic Guards* (p. 294), and *The Governors of the Doelen* by Van der Helst, the so-called *Guards' Peace* by Govert Flinck, *The Governors of the Spinning House* by Karel Dujardin, and the *View of the IJ outside Amsterdam* by Willem van der Velde the Younger. From the former Admiralty of Zeeland a portrait of De Ruyter by Bol (p. 292) came to increase the collection.

On 25th August 1808 Cornelis Apostool, a much-travelled dilettante and former diplomat, was appointed Director of the Royal Museum. He carried out his task most excellently.

The idea was that the Royal Museum should not only contain old works of art but also stimulate the work of living painters. For this purpose some rooms of the palace were reserved for exhibitions. By 15th September 1808 the museum and exhibition rooms were able to receive the public. It was a very great success. In 1809 once again an exhibition of works by Dutch contemporaries was held and several works were bought for the museum, among others the fine *View in the Park of Saint Cloud* by Pieter Rudolph Kleyn (p. 269).

In the meantime Apostool was on the look-out all over the country for desirable paintings. Thus in November 1809 he saw the collection of F. J. O. Boymans at Utrecht but did not advise buying it *en bloc*, as the owner hoped, because in his opinion it contained too much of indifferent or even poor quality. However the collection of A. L. Gevers, page to King Louis and heir to the select cabinet of Adriaan Leonard van Heteren was taken over in its entirety for about one hundred thousand guilders. Once again, the 137 items were mainly works from the Golden Age of the Netherlands. Among them were famous pieces such as *The Feast of St Nicolas* (p. 289) and *The Parrot's Cage* (p. 237) by Jan Steen, Ter Borch's so-called *Paternal Advice* (p. 295, where it is titled 'Group in an Interior'), *The Ox-Drove* by Claes Berchem, *The View of the Martyr's Canal at Amsterdam* (The Martelaarsgracht) by Jan van der Heyden (p. 297) and *The Breakfast* by Gabriël Metsu. The collection included, moreover, a number of Flemish works, the most important piece being a sketch for a dramatic *Procession to Calvary* (p. 139) by Rubens, and finally, one or two works of later date. It is interesting to find here also one primitive painting which was once again erroneously attributed to Van Eyck: an *Adoration of the Kings*.

In the same year that these paintings were acquired Apostool completed the first catalogue of the Royal Museum. In it he described 459 paintings, as well as a number of antiquarian objects and some fifty drawings.

Soon however the museum's period of prosperity came to an end. In 1810 Louis Napoleon resigned the throne and the Kingdom of Holland was incorporated into France. There was no longer any money for purchases. The paintings remained undisturbed where they were. They were still at the palace when the Prince of Orange, the son of William V who had died in 1806, made his joyous entry in December 1813 into Amsterdam after it had been liberated from the French and, in his turn, settled down in the former town hall. Apostool was still in charge of the collection.

Now a change occurred. King William I did not want the museum to stay in the palace. The rooms, not easy to reach, had never been very suitable for the purpose. The aim was now to find the collection its own home, as had indeed been attempted earlier. The home was found in the Trippenhuis at the Kloveniersburgwal. It was a stately, very monumental building, erected in the years 1660–1662, and had been commissioned by the brothers Louis and Hendrik Trip, gun-founders and dealers in Swedish iron. It already had a connection with the fine arts: we mentioned in passing that C. S. Roos had installed exhibition rooms in it in 1798 for the works of living artists. In 1808 the State had bought its northern half to establish the Royal Institute there, while the Legislative Body also used it. The southern section belonged to the city of Amsterdam, having been bequeathed to it in 1771. In 1815, therefore, the museum moved to the northern half of the Trippenhuis. After the interior had been somewhat altered, it was opened in February 1817 as the Rijksmuseum. There was not much space. Moreover room had to be made for the Print Room, and sharing accommodation with the Royal Academy, the successor of the Royal Institute, which had been moved to the southern half, was no undivided pleasure, as it also eventually began to complain of lack of space. In addition, the light in the Trippenhuis was far from being ideal for a museum. But for the time being these hardships were not so very serious.

King William I in his turn showed interest in the museum. It was thanks to him that in the first years of his reign some fine purchases could be recorded, such as Wouwerman's *Kicking White Horse;* Govert Flinck's *Portrait of Vondel;* Frans Hals' *Jolly Toper* (p. 151) and – a curious example of the taste of the time – Moreelse's *Beautiful Shepherdess*; there were also, *The Pantry* (p. 239) by De Hooch, *The Waterfall* by Jacob van Ruijsdael, Jan Steen's *Self-portrait* (p. 289), *The Cheerful Fiddler* by Gerard Honthorst, *Dreaming* (p. 207) by Maes, a *Self-portrait* by Troost; and various other works. To this impressive list of acquisitions was added the first legacy the Rijksmuseum received, twenty-two portraits from Mrs. Balguérie, née van Rijswijk (1823). Thus the first fifteen years after French domination was a flourishing period for the Rijksmuseum. Unfortunately a period of stagnation followed, a result of the Belgian war and its consequences. Owing to a chronic shortage of money many a masterpiece eluded the Rijksmuseum in those following years. The omissions of the period caused irreparable harm to the national art estate, for much of what should have stayed in the Netherlands left the country for good. After 1830 only two purchases are worth mentioning, both of them made by King William I for the museum from his own funds: *The Egg Dance* by Pieter Aertsz and *The Night Banquet* by Joos van Winghe (in 1839).

Cornelis Apostool died in 1844, over eighty years old, after a directorship of more than thirty-five years. His successor, the painter Jan Willem Pieneman, who was also Director of the Academy of Fine Arts, only remained in office for three years and he had no successor. For thirty years the Rijksmuseum had to make do with a governing body. In the narrow sense, it faithfully discharged its task but during this period the museum can hardly be said to have been truly alive. When the excellent collection of the late King William II was auctioned at The Hague in 1850, (eight Rembrandts, Flemish Primitives, Italian art, etc.), the Rijksmuseum acquired nothing! The Louvre and the Wallace Collection in London now display what eluded the Netherlands then. From this whole period only one acquisition need be mentioned: *The Portrait of a Man and his Wife* (pp. 152–3) by Frans Hals which was bought in 1852 for the very moderate price of Fls. 530.

When Louis Napoleon founded the Royal Museum in 1808, he had, as we have seen, given orders for the former National Art Gallery to be transferred to Amsterdam. Some of the paintings and art objects, however, remained in the house on the Binnenhof at The Hague to which they were taken in 1805. In the next ten years nothing happened to them. But when the Battle of Waterloo had made an end of Napoleon's empire for good, it was decided that the works of art which the French had stolen in Europe at the time should be returned to their rightful owners. A commission was put in charge of fetching back what belonged to the Netherlands and Belgium. With great trouble and despite violent resistance on the part of the French, the members managed to get inside the Louvre on 19th September 1815, under the protection of Allied troops thanks to Wellington's intervention. On their instructions, soldiers removed from the walls the paintings from Holland, but sixty-eight were missing, among them some important ones. The majority of these still hang in French museums. With great joy the country received back its art treasures. In The Hague the paintings were first of all taken to the building where Prince William V's cabinet had previously been established. On 1st May 1816 the King appointed as Director of the 'Royal Cabinet of Paintings' the collector Jonkheer Johan Steengracht van Oost-Capelle (1782–1846), and as Deputy-Director the painter Jan Willem Pieneman. They received 133 paintings under their management, almost all of them from the cabinet of William V. Seven pictures from elsewhere were added to them and eight modern canvases which His Majesty had bought shortly before. In contrast to the dual purpose of the Rijksmuseum, this collection took little account of the historical importance of its items.

For several years people looked for suitable premises for the museum. In 1820 these were found at last, in the old Mauritshuis, an intimate building of a stateliness and distinction worthy of the collections of the princes and moreover in a position as easily accessible as it was picturesque. After a few structural alterations, the cabinet of paintings was transferred there in August 1821. It was allocated the first floor, whilst on the lower floor was the Royal Cabinet of Curiosities. As in the Trippenhuis, therefore, accommodation had to be shared, and in the long run this raised difficulties. But for the time being there was no trouble. King William I, who generally lived at The Hague, took even more interest in the Mauritshuis than in the Rijksmuseum. He enriched the collection with many purchases, as had his father in the eighteenth century, if not always with such happy results. One splendid achievement, however, was the acquisition of Vermeer's *View of Delft* (pp. 248–9) in 1822 and, in 1828, Rembrandt's *Anatomy Lesson of Dr Nicolaes Tulp* (p. 290). The Vermeer had really first been noted by Apostool and Steengracht had not been in favour of the purchase. It must have been still more galling for the Amsterdam director that his museum missed the typically Amsterdam group-portrait by Rembrandt, although the money for it came largely from the proceeds of a recent sale of inferior paintings from the Rijksmuseum.

A year later the popular *NELRI-series,* so-called from the first letters of the Latin titles of the five pastels (see p. 303) by Cornelis Troost made its entry into the Mauritshuis. Apart from old works of art, William I also bought modern paintings. When these numbered about 150 in 1838, they were transferred from the Mauritshuis to Haarlem, where a separate museum for nineteenth-century art was founded in the Pavilion Welgelegen. It existed until 1884 when its collections were added to the new, large Rijksmuseum in Amsterdam. Since 1838 the Royal Cabinet has no longer contained modern works. After the Belgian War, the Mauritshuis, too, entered a long period of stagnation. A not very fortunate purchase in 1832 ended the period of expansion for forty-three years.

Rotterdam got its museum later than Amsterdam and The Hague. Its foundation came about differently from those of the Rijksmuseum and the Mauritshuis.

At the beginning of the nineteenth century there lived in Utrecht a somewhat eccentric collector, Frans Jacob Otto Boymans (1767–1847) who certainly possessed some valuable paintings together with many of doubtful quality. In the town rumours went around of drastic restorations which he had effected on spoiled canvases and of 'improvements' which some signatures might have received. This gossip does not seem to have been totally unfounded but most people did not know what was true and what was not, as the owner acted rather mysteriously where his treasures were concerned. Whether Boymans really was an art-expert was not clear but what is certain is that he liked to be thought one. One gets the impression that criticism had made him suspicious of the world because he did not feel certain of himself. He seems to have been the personification of hurt vanity.

Portrait of Cornelis Ploos van Amstel, 1766,
by Jacobus Buys (1724–1801).
Panel. 57 × 44.5 cm. (22$^{1}/_{2}$" × 17$^{1}/_{2}$"). Rijksmuseum No. 667.

Exceedingly proud of his collections, he conceived the plan of leaving his paintings to a museum which for all time would bear his name. The town of Utrecht had already had the chance of obtaining Boymans' collection during his lifetime but friction with the Burgomaster, Van Asch van Wijck, who presumably knew all too well the rumours current about the collection, made it impossible for this plan to be carried out. Just as these negotiations failed, Boymans received a visit from an old friend of his student days, M. C. Bichon van IJsselmonde, Burgomaster of Rotterdam. Rotterdam, then the third town of the Netherlands, did not possess a museum. Burgomaster Bichon realised the importance of having one but could not afford to be fastidious. In absolute secrecy he agreed with Boymans that Rotterdam be heir to the collection, and that the town for its part would provide a suitable museum building. That is what happened. Shortly after Boymans had made his promise, in 1841, the fine old Administrative Building for the drainage of the Schieland area was bought. At that time Rotterdam itself owned only eleven paintings.

After Boymans' death in 1847, the Rotterdam art dealer Arnoldus Lamme went to Utrecht in order to value the collection that had been left, aided by his son Arie Johannes. They established that it contained no fewer than 1193 paintings! These were stored as in a warehouse, in piles against the walls of five rooms in Boymans' house, in the stable and in the attic. For a long time there had been no room left to hang everything. Furthermore some thousands of drawings were included and a quantity of European and Asiatic porcelain.

Only 239 pieces were considered to be suitable for museum purposes, but that number was increased later. Still in that same year, everything was transferred to Rotterdam and on 3rd July 1849 the Boymans Museum in Schieland House was opened. The two Lammes became managers. What could be considered the dregs of the paintings and art books were auctioned in 1853 and subsequent years; the proceeds formed a welcome fund for acquisitions.

In these auctions lies part of the reason why we remain in the dark as regards the much criticised quality of the Boymans collection. The other reason is the great fire which ravaged the museum in 1864. Much of the original collection was then lost: a small portrait of a woman by Rembrandt of approximately 1632, which must however have been in bad condition, a fine Frans Hals, seven works by Aelbert Cuyp and two by Jan Steen, a *View of the Castle at Bentheim* by Jacob van Ruijsdael, a Philips Koninck, a Potter, eleven Moreelses, a Frans van Mieris, a Van der Neer, two Ter Borchs and much else. Of the eleven pieces from the old possessions of the town which hung in the Museum as well, six were burned. Also serious was the loss of a large family group by Carel Fabritius which had been bought in 1860 and of a beautiful Van der Helst, representing Rijckloff van Goens and his family. But fortunately important pieces were saved. The rebuilding of Schieland House, tackled parsimoniously, was completed in 1867. The insurance money was used to replenish the collection in Boymans' spirit. This was not always a success but at least Rotterdam acquired a museum which it would probably not have had so soon but for the initiative and ambition of an out-of-town man.

Following the example of the large towns, the municipal council of Haarlem decided to found a museum on 8th August 1860. It was based on the *Repasts* (see pp. 148–9, 283) by Frans Hals and others which, since the closing of the Doelens, had hung in the town hall. To these the paintings from the hospitals and other municipal institutions were added. It was only when all these works were brought together in one building that it became clear what an enormous wealth of art-treasures Haarlem possessed. The quality of this core of the collection has never been equalled by later purchases. In the town hall a number of rooms were prepared for the museum; on 30th June 1862 they were ready to receive the public. It had not been necessary to go to a lot of expense on this account; nevertheless the result was impressive.

PRIVATE INITIATIVE AND OFFICIAL ACTIVITY

There came a lull in the activities of the Dutch museums. This could not be attributed only to the financial crisis caused by the Belgian war for this was overcome in the 1840s. The cause should rather be sought in the principles of the liberal state, in which private enterprise reigned supreme and the authorities wished to limit their own activities to a minimum. There was plenty of interest in anything concerning the past, the literature of all Europe was full of it. In the Netherlands, Potgieter even wrote a copious essay bearing the title *The Rijksmuseum* (1844). But however intensive the interest in history and the old masters it benefited the museums very little, owing to the attitude of most lovers of Antiquities in the Romantic Period. A person like Potgieter did not know how to *look*. An old painting immediately stirred his thoughts, bringing all kinds of matters of historical interest to his mind and setting his pen in motion, which then took its own free course without his eyes being involved. His country's past served him and his like as a source of patriotic inspiration – a noble purpose indeed, which meant much to national self-respect – but men who looked at art in this manner could hardly grow into connoisseurs!

This does not mean that there were no connoisseurs. No less than before, the Netherlands collected paintings, but this was not done primarily by the museums. Purchases of significance were only made by the private collectors. There was the industrialist from Dordrecht, Leendert Dupper (1799–1870) who in 1850 had inherited an important collection of paintings by seventeenth-century masters from his uncle Johannes Rombouts, which he increased considerably. Dupper's preference tended toward the landscape. His collection contained wonderful examples of Jan van Goyen's art. He also liked arcadian scenes painted by the Italianisers. The collection which he bequeathed to the State of the Netherlands, to be placed in the Rijksmuseum, contained sixty-four paintings (apart from the Van Goyens already mentioned) by Ostade, Jan Steen, Dou and Maes, for instance.

Another interesting collector was Daniël Franken Dzn (1838–1898), a sensitive Amsterdam art-expert and antiquarian who started his career in the banking world. His speciality was Dutch prints of the

51

early Golden Age but he also collected paintings from this period. He died a bachelor and left the Rijksmuseum a large sum of money for purchases, in addition to his paintings, drawings and prints.

By far the most important collector was the great Amsterdam banker Adriaan van der Hoop (1778–1854). He was most interested, like Dupper, in the work of the Dutch painters of the Golden Age. In this field, Van der Hoop outpaced all other Dutch collectors. His greatest purchases were Rembrandt's *Jewish Bride* (pp. 200–1), which he acquired in 1834 from the London art dealer J. Smith, and *The Woman in Blue, Reading a Letter* (p. 296) by Vermeer. Round these peaks were grouped four De Hoochs, five Jan Steens, two Hobbemas, the *Portrait of Marie Voogt Claesdr* (p. 283) by Frans Hals, *The Mill* (p. 299) by Ruijsdael, and, furthermore, exquisite works by Metsu, Dou, Brekelenkam, Saenredam, the two Berckheydes, Wouwerman, Potter, Adriaen van de Velde, Hackaert, Lingelbach and Pynacker, the *Italian Landscape with Sketchers* by Both (p. 159), *The Cannon Shot* by Willem van de Velde and many other works. He also bought paintings by Rubens, Van Dyck and Teniers, as well as some foreign masters from the same period. On the other hand, he possessed no 'Primitives' and he had hardly anything from the eighteenth century. When the collector of these fine paintings died childless, he left them all to the town of Amsterdam. The town considered itself unable to pay the death duties, however, which was its obligation under Dutch law, and these were in fact paid by some of its more public-spirited citizens, in particular Jacob de Vos Izn. Thus Amsterdam came to possess the most brilliant nineteenth-century Dutch collection of paintings.

The following is another example of private initiative. In 1863 the fiftieth anniversary of the Kingdom of the Netherlands was to be commemorated. Art-lovers in Amsterdam who were aware of the complaints about the highly inadequate accommodation which the Trippenhuis afforded their finest art-treasures, had the idea of marking this occasion by founding a new building for the Rijksmuseum, a temple worthy of the national arts. Potgieter's words would in this way be transformed into deeds. A 'Commission to prepare the Establishment of an Art-Museum' was formed (1862) with the zealous author and antiquarian Alberdingk Thijm as its secretary, and among its members the writers Jacob van Lennep and W. J. Hofdijk, the history painter Charles Rochussen, the collector Jacob de Vos Izn. The government in The Hague initially indicated its approval of the scheme.

The plan was that a large building should be erected in which the collections from the Trippenhuis could be combined with the Van der Hoop Museum, which since the death of the testator had existed as a separate institution. In this new museum, moreover, several other collections also of an antiquarian nature could be concentrated. It would therefore be planned to show two things: Dutch art, and objects of historical interest, side by side – or rather, linked together to make a wonderful synthesis; this was the ideal of the middle of the nineteenth century. In imitation of the former Musée Napoléon in Paris, and in honour of the jubilee celebrations, the name of 'William I Museum' was proposed. The Commission drew up a programme for an architectural competition which, completely in the spirit of the time, stipulated that the building should be monumental in design with a high, well-lighted entrance-hall or gallery, containing a colossal statue of King William I, while other brave and talented Dutchmen, who had helped in the liberation of 1813, would be honoured by busts, plaques or inscriptions. They stipulated that brick, the national product, was to be the building material.

The result was disappointing and none of the designs submitted was approved. A plan by Messrs Lange of Munich was admittedly given an award, but Dutch national feeling could not wax passionate over a building with columns in Ionic and Doric style – very unsuited to Amsterdam. Moreover this project was too small and too expensive. 'We must found', argued the Committee, 'not a freestone temple, but a Dutch museum of paintings.' The Roermond architect P. J. H. Cuypers was the second to receive an award for his design.

The Commission also made an effort to collect the money required. The amount was to be made up by the State, but this was never done. Neither the Minister, Thorbecke, nor his successors appeared prepared 'in these expensive times', about which they complained, to place on the budget an item for the building of the museum. Thus the efforts of the Amsterdam people remained fruitless and the jubilee year of 1863 passed without anything being achieved. Efforts made in the following years were equally unsuccessful. When in 1870 the Rijksmuseum accepted the Dupper legacy, the lack of space in the Trippenhuis became worse than ever, especially as the Royal Academy had absorbed even more of its rooms.

At last, in 1872, fresh initiative was taken by the Amsterdam citizens and this led to Parliament (at the suggestion of one of its members, Van Houten) including a memorandum for the museum plan during the discussions on the 1873 budget. By this time the principle that the establishment of the museum was a matter for the Government had been accepted. Amsterdam now gave a site, as well as a contribution of Fls. 100,000 to the cost of building. Moreover the city promised to put its unrivalled possessions of portrait-groups of the Civic Guards and other old paintings, its antiquities and the Van der Hoop Museum at the disposal of the large Rijksmuseum on permanent loan. A new commission, presided over by Burgomaster Den Tex, now got to work on the project.

The challenged Lange design could be put aside with an easy conscience as its author had meanwhile died; after a lot of discussion Cuypers received the commission in 1876. It is not surprising, since he had followed all the planning from such close quarters (he was a brother-in-law of Alberdingk Thijm), that in his final project he retained many elements of the design as it had been formulated in 1862. Thus the new Rijksmuseum became a typical example of the ideas of the middle of the nineteenth century with their predilection for history, as practised by Potgieter and Thijm, in fact it was the most monumental example of these ideas in the Netherlands. The most glorious moments of national history were almost completely expressed. A number of Cuyper's rooms were copied from outstanding Dutch buildings of the Romanesque and Gothic periods (sometimes, for practical reasons, in reduced size). Decorative pictures showing scenes from history covered the walls of the front hall; great artists, musicians and men of letters glittered in the coloured, but predominantly grey, windows which had been manufactured in England; the plaques and names that had been desired in 1862 were carved on the façade which was also enlivened by tile tableaux extolling the nation's past. There were so many of them that they acquired for the Rijksmuseum the disrespectful nickname of 'the building with the sticky labels'. The Bible and Vondel were quoted in places where it seemed appropriate and Alberdingk Thijm furnished an inscription in verse. So anybody approaching the building was immediately greeted by a display of patriotic sentiments. In 1885 it was inaugurated with great solemnity. The picture-section had by then been installed; the time-consuming arrangement of arts and crafts was completed in subsequent years.

The two-fold intention of the founders of the museum was reflected in the numerous purchases and donations which thereafter, under the successive Directors General F. D. O. Obreen and Jonkheer B. W. F. van Riemsdijk, came to enrich the Rijksmuseum: pieces of both aesthetic and historic importance were acquired. But while the new methods of art-historical research, in which Obreen has made his career, began to show remarkable results, the study of works of historic interest gradually moved into the background. The duality of history and art was broken in favour of a move towards purely aesthetic interests and the road towards a new period had begun.

In the years when Amsterdam was struggling for the new Rijksmuseum there was also a revival of interest in the Mauritshuis. This was not due to the Director, Jonkheer J. K. J. de Jonge, whose proper profession was that of Secretary of the First Chamber of the States-General and Assistant Master of the Rolls, so much as to the energetic and all-powerful Permanent Secretary of Arts and Sciences, Jonkheer Victor de Stuers. In 1873 – the same year as that in which the Rijksmuseum had appeared for the first time as an item in the budget – he wrote in *De Gids* (*The Guide*), Potgieter's old periodical, a sharp article entitled 'Holland at its Narrowest', in which he violently criticised the tepid spirit of the authorities regarding the old monuments. Two years later he was installed as the first Permanent Secretary of the newly created Arts and Sciences section of the Ministry of the Interior. As leading official expert on the antiquarian property of the country, he immediately began to interest himself in everything within his purview. He furthered the building of the Rijksmuseum with all his strength, its purchasing policy carrying his stamp for many years.

In the Mauritshuis things were handled in the same manner. The collections were sorted under his personal direction. Stored away they found important portraits and other works which had lain undisplayed since its foundation. In order to make room, De Stuers arranged, in 1875, that the Royal Cabinet of Curiosities should be moved, so that the whole building could be freed for the paintings. He himself undertook the preparation of a new catalogue. And for the first time in forty-three years money was again made available for purchases. When in 1889 a fully qualified Director was found in the person of the highly competent Abraham Bredius, the Mauritshuis was definitely redeemed from its term of inactivity.

Abraham Bredius was a native of Amsterdam, descended from a family of well-to-do merchants. By studying industriously he had made himself the leading expert of his generation on the Dutch old masters. He had travelled and had acquired the necessary museum experience in the Rijksmuseum where, from 1880 to 1889, he had occupied the post of Deputy-Director of the Netherlands Museum for Sculpture and Applied Arts. Originally he had favoured the Rijksmuseum with presents, especially paintings by little-known Dutch artists. During his time at the Hague, until 1909, and even thereafter, he lent many pictures from his fantastic private collection of Rembrandts and other old masters to the Mauritshuis. The highlight was the *Saul and David* (p. 195), a canvas Bredius had bought at the Rembrandt Exhibition in Amsterdam in 1898.

Among the numerous acquisitions which enriched the museum during his period of office, the following are most worthy of mention: Rembrandt's *Rest during the Flight to Egypt*, a fine *Moonlight* by Aert van der Neer, the tender *Young Girl* (p. 245) by Vermeer and the large vase of *Flowers* (p. 130) which is the masterpiece of Ambrosius Bosschaert (both of them bequests by A. A. des Tombe, 1903); a legacy of seven paintings by Dr T. Blom Coster (1904), containing among other things portraits by Govert Flinck, Cornelis de Vos and Adriaen Hanneman; the Singendonck bequest (1907) consisting of family portraits; a landscape by Frans Post (a gift from P. J. van Dokkum of Utrecht, 1906) and a small Jacob van Ruisdael (from Dr C. Hofstede de Groot, 1909). This is but a small sample of many acquisitions. In this period purchases kept pace with legacies and donations. There were the fine *Goldfinch* (p. 205) by Carel Fabritius, still-lifes by Kalf and Fijt, landscapes by Salomon van Ruysdael and Jan Vermeer of Delft and the two charming small portraits of George van der Mijn. Moreover countless loans, which the director was able to effect through his personal connections, enriched the museum for longer or shorter periods, so that something new was always to be seen there. Bredius' policy was successfully continued by his successor Professor W. Martin.

Although the Haarlem museum had been well provided with works by the local school since its foundation there were still gaps in its collections. It could hardly be otherwise in a town so richly endowed with native art-masterpieces. In addition it was especially art historians such as Bredius and Hofstede de Groot and Haarlem people like A. J. Enschedé who brought these gaps to light. In order to fill them, a separate society was formed, 'The Society for the Extension of the Collection of Art and Antiquities in the Frans Hals Museum'. Year after year it donated one or more pieces from the Haarlem School. Often these were works by minor masters difficult or impossible to find elsewhere. In addition, there were loans from the Rijksmuseum and the Mauritshuis and legacies from A. J. Enschedé, D. Franken Dzn and, in 1926, from C. J. Gonnet. The important portraits which the museum received have already been mentioned. The Frans Hals Museum has thus been enormously enriched. Not only does it now contain some of the highlights by Jan van Scorel, Frans Hals, Verspronck and De Bray; it has also become one of the best collections of the Haarlem School, in the widest sense of the word – a real El Dorado for those who are interested in art-history as well as art for its own sake.

The spirit of initiative which Amsterdam gave the Rijksmuseum and which Victor de Stuers and Bredius represented in The Hague, was for the time being not felt in the Rotterdam museum. The Directors – A. J. Lamme from 1847–1870, Dirk A. Lamme from 1870–1878, F. D. O. Obreen from 1878–1883 (after that he became the first Director General of the Rijksmuseum) and P. Haverkorn van Rijsewijk, 1884–1908 – initially used the limited budget at their disposal mainly to purchase paintings, mostly smaller ones, by Rotterdam artists. They considered the museum in the first place as a local institution and only in the second place as a national one. In view of the means at their disposal, this was a wise conception, for their financial limitations in the nineteenth century were severe, not to say short-sighted. Just as Utrecht had once declined Boymans' collection and afterwards missed the one belonging to Florent van Ertborn, which later was to become the basis of the rich Antwerp Museum, so Rotterdam missed its opportunity when in 1845 the highly important Verstolk van Soelen collection was bequeathed to the town: it was rejected in order to save the death duties! The same thing happened in 1869 with the Vis Blokhuyzen collection. This weak attitude was afterwards deeply regretted.

In addition the paintings of the local school, the national – even somewhat internationally flavoured – collection which formed the basis of the museum was extended as far as possible by works of other Dutch painters, the vast majority of them from the seventeenth century and from the nineteenth when the museum was founded. Interest was directed in particular towards works of the Hague School which were then easy to obtain. For years on end the Annual Reports, which started in 1879, reflect this attitude. The donations and legacies to the museum were similar in character. On the whole they were not of very great value. In contrast with Amsterdam, private enterprise in the Rotterdam of those days did not greatly concern itself with the fine arts. When in 1893 for the first time a work by J. B. Jongkind was bought from England, the 'Dutch' quality of the collection was still preserved, because although the painter spent most of his life in France, he was in fact born Dutch, and this picture was painted in Holland in about 1854: it shows a moonlit view of Overschie (near Rotterdam).

Obreen and Haverkorn van Rijsewijk, besides looking after the collections, concentrated their efforts on increasing (during their probably abundant leisure) their knowledge of the paintings under their care. They regularly incorporated their findings in their Annual Reports, art-historical documents of lasting value. They also kept in touch with colleagues in other towns. In 1887 mention is made for the first time of advice given by Bredius. The steady work of the two Directors gradually bore fruit. The 'lean years' came ton an end. Towards the turn of the century the Boymans Museum began to attract the attention of wider circles, to blossom out into an institution of more than merely local importance.

NEW PATHS

Not many years had elapsed since the inauguration of the new Rijksmuseum before criticism of it began to arise. It came from a younger generation who approached art from a different angle. The aesthetic value of a work of art, not its historic significance, was important to them. They lived for beauty, not for the antiquarian content of these exquisite testimonies of the past; they advocated the enjoyment of the eye–or of the soul, if one prefers–not the appeal to reason. In literature these concepts had already broken through in 1880 in the utterances of the young, enthusiastic authors who became known as 'the Eighties Group'.

In addition, in spite of its size, the building, from shortly after its opening, had not provided sufficient space. During and shortly after its construction sizable legacies had been received, of which little or no account had been taken beforehand; in 1877 and 1903 a large series of family portraits from Jonkheer Jacob de Witte van Citters; in 1880 the collection containing fifty-two items of Jonkheer J. S. H. van de Poll; in 1881 the legacy of forty-four portraits bequeathed by the Dowager van Winter, née Bicker; in 1885 the Liotard legacy of thirty-five works; in 1898 some forty paintings from the G. de Clerq collection, and so on. Thus discontent reigned about the museum. The fact that only thirteen years after its opening, modernisations were thought necessary, was not in itself surprising. The planning had taken a long time; the original conceptions of 1861 had admittedly been expanded but many of the old ideas had nevertheless remained. Hence, as is often the case in such large enterprises, the new building was completed, the latest ideas were not been included in it.

On the occasion of the celebrations to mark the accession of Queen Wilhelmina in 1898, an exhibition of Rembrandt's works had been organised in the Amsterdam Municipal Museum. It was a most spectacular display. Although art-historians have since denied the authenticity of some of the paintings then catalogued as being by the master, it remains a fact that the public has never before or since been able to see so many of his works together. The Rijksmuseum co-operated by lending *The Nightwatch,* among others. In the Municipal Museum it was hung in a room with a side light (from the south). The visitors came, as it were, unawares on the radiant beauty of the masterpiece. Nobody had seen Holland's greatest painting in this way before – not in the dark Trippenhuis, nor in the new Rijksmuseum where Cuypers had installed the canvas on the first floor as the culminating point at the end of the middle axis which formed the 'Gallery of Honour', against the south wall, where it received the light from the north through the glass ceiling, in so far as this was not intercepted by the towers of the building with their high roofs. The placing of the painting was well thought out and intellectually responsible but fell short aesthetically. And it was on this very aesthetic element that the new conceptions of art laid full stress. When the painting returned to its old position after the exhibition, the desire for a place more in conformity with the new requirements continued. The argument for modernisation was fairly soon won. In 1901 the Queen appointed a preparatory commission. Behind the museum a shed was erected whose main axis ran parallel with that of the building and *The Nightwatch* was transferred to it. An ingenious arrangement of windows and hatches made it possible to study all kinds of lighting on the canvas.

The result of the enquiry was expressed in a lengthy report, in which it was established that a position with a side light from the south-west was ideal for *The Nightwatch*. The next step was the realisation of this wish. It was decided to construct at the back of the museum, as a continuation of the 'Gallery of Honour', a room of about 26 ft. by 36 ft. which would satisfy these requirements. The task of executing it was given to the architect of the museum, Cuypers. At the meetings of the Commission the old master builder had raised no objections to the plan for building a new *Nightwatch* room. Victor de Stuers alone had been against it. His arguments were that the lighting would hardly be improved and would become more variable, while the great objection to a side light was that only relatively few people at a time would be able to visit the painting in the fairly small room. Later he turned out to have been right.

It was obvious that the outside of the *Nightwatch* extension should be adapted to the façade of the Rijksmuseum. Therefore it was given a decoration in stone relief, on which was depicted a scene showing how Rembrandt was supposed to have painted *The Syndics* (strangely enough not *The Nightwatch!*), surrounded by his pupils. On either side of the passage stood, like sentinels, statues of the master himself and of Frans Hals.

The Ministry of the Interior had agreed with the plan for the *'Nightwatch*-extension' but did not appear prepared to bear the cost except to a very limited extent. In The Hague it was argued that the initiative had come from the citizens of Amsterdam and that they, therefore, would have to bear two-thirds of the financial consequences, i. e. an amount of Fls. 28,000. The lion's share of this, Fl. 20,000, came from the painter Jozef Israëls. It was the sum which had been collected abroad in honour of his seventy-fifth birthday. Bredius, always liberal where museum matters were concerned, undertook to provide the greater part of the balance. The *'Nightwatch*-extension' was opened on 16th July 1906, the day on which Rembrandt's tercentenary was commemorated. Amsterdam celebrated the occasion in great style; it was hardly less solemn than the inauguration of the Rijksmuseum itself in 1885. Just as Johannes Bosboom, as the most honoured Dutch artist living at the time had unveiled *The Nightwatch,* so Israëls now acted as the doyen of the painters.

This was characteristic of the change in taste wich had occurred. Although only five years younger than Bosboom, Israëls was ahead of him as an artist by almost a generation, for Bosboom, who had started his career as an illustrator of national history, had never in his later impressionistic-style paintings of church interiors quite lost the feeling for the old historical Dutch Calvinist atmosphere, while Jozef Israëls in his fishermen-scenes and interiors of the village of Laren, it is true, had retained the romantic element, but did not feel nostalgia for the past. He had no ambition to become, so to speak, a painter-lecturer on national history. Therefore he stood, more than Bosboom, on the threshold of a new period.

The *'Nightwatch*-extension' meant the beginning of a break with the domination of the historical idea. But in addition it meant a break with the idea that a work of art, once it has received its place in the pantheon of national glory, will have to occupy it till the end of time. The static museum gradually began to turn into something more dynamic. This was to be the beginning of a movement of gathering momentum.

The idea that art's main interest is historical was replaced by a new valuation based on artistic merits alone; this paved the way for an appreciation of other art besides that of the Golden Age, on which, as we have seen, interest in the Netherlands had for a long time been almost exclusively concentrated. What Iconoclasm had left of medieval art was little valued, because it lacked the characteristics of the 'national' in the sense of 'bourgeois', Protestant, trading republic. But for similarly patriotic reasons in Belgium and Germany since the Romantic age the pictorial art of the Primitives had been held in esteem; there the Gothic masters did recall the glorious national past of Flanders and Brabant, of Cologne, Nuremberg, the Hanseatic towns and those along the Danube. It was only much later that Dutch art-historians came to realise that the work of their own medieval painters and sculptors was in no way inferior to that in surrounding countries. Scholars from abroad sometimes pointed the way. Only when this realisation penetrated did Dutch museums begin to make room for the period which the brothers Boisserée in Germany and Florent van Ertborn in Belgium had admired so deeply since early in the nineteenth century. The example set by them at last became an incentive to Dutchmen also.

It was not among the paintings of the Rijksmuseum that changes in taste first revealed themselves. Its Director General, Van Riemsdijk, still belonged to the older generation with its strong historic leanings. Neither the purchases of Northern-Netherlandish medieval sculpture nor exhibitions such as that of early religious art in the Netherlands which was organised with the co-operation of many experts in 1913 at 's-Hertogenbosch, met with a wide response in the pictorial section of the Rijksmuseum, apart from a few acquisitions such as Geertgen's

Portrait of Adriaan van der Hoop,
by Jan Adam Kruseman (1804–1862).
Canvas, 125 × 99 cm. (49¹/₄″ × 39″). Rijksmuseum No. 1391.

64

Adoration of the Magi (p. 87), which was bought in 1904. In the Boymans Museum with its much smaller, and hence more flexible, collection, the new spirit manifested itself sooner. There too the museum authorities, as we saw, limited themselves during the nineteenth century to the paintings of the Golden Age, but the interest of the Director Haverkorn van Rijsewijk was eventually aroused by what was happening in the museum world abroad. Thus he relates in the Annual Report for 1904 that the exhibitions held during that year in Siena and London of the works of Simone Martini had convinced him that a painting of Mary with the dead Christ in the Boymans Museum must be by the hand of this artist. Not a little proudly he added that it must therefore be by far the oldest painting in a Dutch museum.

In the same year Haverkorn van Rijsewijk organised, for the first time in his museum, a temporary exhibition of etchings by Jongkind. In subsequent months it was followed by one of reproductions from the first part of the Breviarium Grimani (lent by the Director personally), reproductions of drawings from the Amsterdam Print Room, the second part of the Breviarium Grimani, French prints from the eighteenth century, and drawings and studies by Johannes Bosboom. A very varied programme, by which a new element of life had been introduced into the Rotterdam museum. It was to have a flourishing future.

To the Annual Report for 1902, by way of novelty, a supplement had been added with the names of all those who in the year in question had had a permanent admission-ticket to the Boymans Museum. In 1903 one could read there for the first time the name of the man who in future was to be of great significance to modern museum activities in the Netherlands, F. Schmidt Degener. In 1906 he had apparently not taken out a subscription, but the following Annual Report already mentions his name honourably among the art-historians who visited the museum, and he then appears in one and the same sentence with Bredius, Hofstede de Groot, Moes and other well-known figures. A year later Degener succeeded Haverkorn van Rijsewijk as Director of the Boymans Museum. A new spirit entered the institution!

Frederik Schmidt Degener (1881–1941), a writer of unusual ability, had made a reputation by his studies, while still a young man, especially those on Rembrandt. No less striking than his culture were his taste and breadth of vision in everything he undertook. This appeared immediately on his taking office in Rotterdam. In that very year the collection of the museum was enriched by a foreign painting, *Two Girls* (p. 166) by one of the Le Nain brothers, probably Louis, given by Adolphe Schloss. Thus the principle–or rather the tradition–that Rotterdam limited itself to national art alone, was abandoned. The extension of the collection in an international direction proceeded slowly but steadily, not only with paintings by old masters but in all the fields in which the museum was, or was to become active: sculpture, drawings, prints and various expressions of applied art. As these fall outside our terms of reference, I must pass by purchases such as a fine drawing by Piazzetta, in 1909, but an interior attributed to J. B. S. Chardin and lent to the museum in the following year by J. A. Frederiks may be mentioned. A still-life by Henri Horace Roland de la Porte (formerly attributed to Chardin, cf. p. 302) increased the collection in 1916. It was the first donation D. G. van Beuningen made to the museum; many proofs of his interest in the fine arts were to follow before long. Other acquisitions of foreign origin in these years were a portrait of an abbot by Pietro Longhi (also attributed to Alessandro Longhi or Jacopo Amigoni), bought in 1918, and a sketch after G. B. Tiepolo, representing the martyrdom of St Victor (study for a fresco in the San Satiro at Milan), bought in 1921. Degener himself, before leaving Rotterdam, donated three paintings to the museum by way of a parting gift, among them a large portrait of Margarita de Medici by Justus Sustermans.

Another field now receiving attention was that of the 'Primitives'. Among the changes started by Degener almost immediately after his entrance upon office was the installation of a room specially devoted to this period. The purchase in 1918 of a panel by Jan Provoost representing *The Dispute of St Catherine* (p. 273) with the fifty philosophers, was an important acquisition. But it was natural enough that the main stress should remain on Holland's Golden Age. Works by Aert de Gelder, Adriaen van Ostade, Adriaen Brouwer and several others were acquired. The altruistic help of the Rembrandt Society was also invoked and given regularly so that purchases could be made. In the past this had not been customary in Rotterdam. It was during Degener's directorship too that the Boymans Museum acquired its first work testifying to the hitherto almost unknown talent of a native of Rotterdam, Willem Buytenwech, *Merry Company* (p. 284). It was a donation by a fellow-townsman, A. C. Mees.

In 1922 Schmidt Degener gave up the leadership of the Boymans Museum to become Director General of the Rijksmuseum, as successor to Van Riemsdijk. In the meantime Victor de Stuers had died in 1916. The historical school had now definitely been abandoned and the aesthetic one was given free rein.

Degener's great work in the Rijksmuseum was a complete modernisation of the rooms in accordance with the latest ideas. A thorough sifting for quality made it possible for the paintings to be given much greater space than formerly. In the course of these changes *The Nightwatch* in 1924 moved silently back to its old room but on a better lighted wall than it had previously occupied. In a newly created section for national history were accommodated all those pieces whose historic interest was obviously greater than their artistic one. Works only of significance for art-historians obtained a place in a research section where the specialist could study to his heart's content, without the public being tired by curiosities.

In fact Degener continued in the Rijksmuseum the ideas with which he had begun in Rotterdam. After his appointment as Director General he immediately set himself to acquire foreign works of art. As early as 1922 he bought a portrait of the Venetian senator Vincenzo Zeno by Tintoretto and a sketch of great virtuosity by G. B. Tiepolo, *Telemachus and Mentor* (p. 301). Before long the collection from the Augusteum at Oldenburg offered an extensive opportunity of acquiring more Italian paintings (1923–1924, with the generous co-operation of the Rembrandt Society and private support). Afterwards numerous Italian paintings were added, mainly thanks to the large Kessler-Hülsmann bequest in 1940. As a result of a donation by Sir Henry Deterding in 1936, the first two Venetian views by Francesco Guardi (p. 301) made their entry into the museum's collection.

From the Spanish School a large *Bodega* by Alejandro de Loarte was obtained in 1922 (a donation by a group of members of the Rembrandt Society). A portrait of the Marchioness De Llano by Anton Raphaël Mengs was received from B. de Geus van den Heuvel in 1939 and in 1933 D. G. van Beuningen donated a fine, small El Greco of *Christ crucified* (p. 282) against a background showing Toledo. By far the most important acquisition of the Spanish School was, however, the portrait of *Don Ramon Satue* (p. 271), a late, mature masterpiece by Goya of 1823 (bought in 1922 with the aid of the Rembrandt Society).

Some French paintings were also acquired. The 'Primitives' section was extended by a group by Jacob Cornelisz van Oostsanen (in 1923); a triptych by the Master of Delft (donation by J. H. van Heek, 1933); *St Jerome* by Marinus van Reymerswaele (bought with the help of the Rembrandt Society and the National Aid Fund, 1933) and two small altar wings by the Master of Brunswick (Kessler-Hülsmann bequest, 1940). To these were added, from the period of the Renaissance, the highly impressive portraits of *Sir Thomas Gresham* (p. 117) and his wife (bought in 1931 with the help of the Rembrandt Society).

In the meantime there were also acquisitions of Dutch seventeenth-century paintings. M. P. Voûte donated three biblical scenes by Barent Fabritius and, through a provision in his will made possible the acquisition of Verspronck's charming *Girl in Blue* (p. 285) in 1928. Degener's most discerning purchase in this field was made in 1926 – *The Country Courtships* (p. 154) by Willem Buytenwech, a painter he had admired when at Rotterdam. In 1936 Sir Henry Deterding made some princely donations to the Rijksmuseum, which included *The Little Street* (p. 247) by Vermeer and excellent works by Adriaen van Ostade, Jan van Goyen, Aert van der Neer, Jan van de Capelle, Salomon van Ruysdael, Nicolaes Maes and Jan van der Heyden. Now more and more Degener's interest began to move again towards the great Dutchmen of the seventeenth-century. He acquired the tenderly painted *Sick Child* (p. 296) by Gabriël Metsu and the well known *Linen Cupboard* (p. 296) by Pieter de Hooch (with the help of the Rembrandt Society and private donors). A landscape by Hercules Seghers (p. 291) was able to make its entry into the Rijksmuseum thanks to an exchange; a large naval painting by Hendrick Cornelisz Vroom, on which one sees East-India vessels sailing away from the Marsdiep, was given by Dr J. W. IJzerman of Wassenaar (in 1930); the Rembrandt Society donated a pen drawing with Dutch ships by Willem van de Velde the Elder, the Photographic Commission a large landscape by Frans Post.

Later in his career, however, Schmidt Degener concentrated chiefly on increasing Rembrandt's representation in the Rijksmuseum, acquiring some extremely important works: the large, burning red *The Denial of St Peter* (p. 291) from the Hermitage at Leningrad; and the *Titus in a Monk's Hood* (p. 290) from Moscow, both of which were bought in 1933 with the aid of the Rembrandt Society; the elaborate portrait of *Rembrandt's Mother as the Prophetess Anna* (p. 290) from the Augusteum at Oldenburg (loaned by M. P. Voûte of Amsterdam in 1922, in 1928 bequeathed by him to the Rembrandt Society and given by it to the museum in the same year); the early panel dating from 1630 with *Jeremiah lamenting the destruction of Jerusalem* (donation by the Rembrandt Society, with the support of private citizens, 1939) and the figure of an eastern potentate (Kessler-Hülsmann bequest, 1940). In 1928 the town of Amsterdam lent the drawing by Rembrandt of his *Anatomy Lesson given by Dr Deyman* which had been damaged by fire.

This flourishing period for the Rijksmuseum came to an end because of the outbreak of the Second World War in 1939 and the death of the Director General in 1941.

In the meantime D. Hannema, who had succeeded Schmidt Degener in Rotterdam, had continued on the road begun by his predecessor. Under his directorship the museum benefited by large donations and legacies which greatly changed its character and made it one of the world's great museums. A very important donation of enamel from Limoges, silver, miniatures, sculptures, drawings and prints offered by Dr A. T. Domela Nieuwenhuis in 1923, suddenly made the Print Room of world-importance, but caused an alarming shortage of space in the old Schieland house. When the collection was swelled by the estate of J. P. van der Schilden who died in 1925 the situation became particularly difficult. Moreover, Dr J. C. J. Bierens de Haan promised his whole, exceedingly sizeable, collection of prints as a legacy for the museum (he died in 1951) and the Montauban van Swijndrecht legacy of 1929 considerably increased the number of drawings and prints.

In 1924, so that the newly acquired works of art could be exhibited, modern art was removed from the building for the time being and exhibited at 8 Van Hogendorpsplein, which had been arranged for this purpose after being vacated by the library shortly before. It was an emergency solution which could only be temporary.

After the necessary preparations, the Municipal Council of Rotterdam decided on 12th April 1928 to found a new museum building. It would be financed by the legacy left to the town some time previously by G. W. Burger. When the plans became known they aroused much enthusiasm among Rotterdam people. Even before a beginning had been made with the new museum, donations began to pour in. Mrs J. A. van Vollenhoven, née van Staveren, for instance, donated a ceiling-decoration by Jacob de Wit.

The commission for the construction was given to A. van der Steur, the town architect of Rotterdam. He designed the new Boymans Museum in the closest collaboration with the Director, Hannema. First of all a small temporary building, in which lighting experiments were carried out with the greatest care, was erected on the site where it was to stand. Afterwards the building progressed quickly. On 6th July 1935 the new Boymans Museum was officially inaugurated. The building satisfied modern concepts; no greater contrast to the Rijksmuseum of Cuypers is imaginable. The element of history which had never been represented in the collections of the Rotterdam museum was completely absent from Van der Steur's design. It was replaced by a purely aesthetic conception, dominated by the requirements of museum practice.

The growth of the collection of paintings in those years proceeded rapidly and the quality became more and more remarkable.

In 1930 Van Beuningen, Goudriaan and Koenigs donated Saenredam's pure, impressive view in the St. Johns' Church at Utrecht and the Amsterdam art-dealer J. Goudstikker gave Ter Borch's rare *Spanish Flagellant Procession* (p. 295). In 1931, thanks to extensive help by the Rembrandt Society and Van Beuningen, Koenigs and Van der Vorm, it was possible to purchase the so-called *Vagabond* (p. 97) by Hieronymus Bosch. Six sketches in oil by Rubens' own hand showing scenes from the life of Achilles found their way in 1933 from the Rubens exhibition at Goudstikker's in Amsterdam to the Rotterdam museum. At the opening of the new building, Franz Koenigs gave a sizeable loan which included four paintings by Bosch (*Saint Christopher* [p. 95], *The Wedding at Cana* and two altar-wings) and four works by Rubens. Later, in 1940, they were to be added to the permanent possessions of the museum. Sir Henry Deterding, who had given Dutch paintings of the highest quality to the Rijksmuseum, did not forget Rotterdam either and in 1931 donated a *Village Feast* by Teniers and a piece by Gerrit Dou which was as subtle as it was detailed–*Young Woman Dressing* (p. 288).

In this period there were purchases of important works by Maerten van Heemskerk (in 1936) and Jean Baptiste Perronneau (in 1937–one having already been obtained in 1924). With the help of the Rembrandt Society, *Blindman's Buff* (p. 256) by Cornelis Troost was bought in 1939. Shortly before the outbreak of the Second World War two superb works by Rembrandt filled a gap in the collections: *Man with a Red Cap* (p. 291) (bought in 1937) and, in 1940, the charming child's head of *Titus* (p. 193), 1655 (both with the aid of the Rembrandt Society and many friends of the arts).

Unlike that of the great museums in Amsterdam and Rotterdam, the character of the Mauritshuis did not change in the twentieth century. The size and atmosphere of the fine old building made this neither possible nor desirable. Activity there was restricted to the constant aim of improving the collection and the way in which it was presented. The acquisitions were, on the whole, limited to Dutch seventeenth-century art, and among them were works of the very highest quality. The most important of these were the *Portrait of the Ensign Loef Vredericx* by Thomas de Keyser (purchased in 1931) (p. 293) and the *Portrait of a Young Man* by Ferdinand Bol (in 1927, with the aid of the Rembrandt Society and private donors). In 1928 Sir Henry Deterding who had remembered the Rijksmuseum and the Boymans

Museum in such a generous manner, gave Gerard ter Borch's exquisite *Lady Writing a Letter* (p. 183) and in 1936 the delicate miniature-like *Girl with Oysters* (p. 288) by Jan Steen, *The Couple* by Frans van Mieris, a *Naval Picture* by Jan van de Capelle and a *Pastoral Scene* by Aelbert Cuyp. J. Goudstikker enriched the collection in 1919 with a sunny Italian landscape by Karel Du Jardin (p. 171).

Occasionally a sixteenth-century painting was bought, in 1920, for instance, a *Resurrection of Christ* by Aelbert Bouts, and in 1939 a *Madonna with Child* by Jan Gossaert. Another purchase slightly outside the normal run was a 'conversation piece' representing the Feytema couple by the late-eighteenth-century painter Wybrandt Hendriks (bought in 1937).

The nature and aims of the Haarlem museum were such that it did not share the growing interest in art from outside the Northern Netherlands. In this local museum works by foreign masters did not seem to be at home. Moreover, money for purchases was only available on a very limited scale. But this did not mean that it was a dead collection. To overcome the serious lack of space caused by the gradual extension of the collections and to make possible a new, more aesthetically appealing display, attempts were made to find other accomodation. This was found in the former Old Men's Home bought by the town in 1906. The architect L. C. Dumont made the necessary alterations, and on 14th May 1913 the new, larger home of the museum, which now bore the name of Frans Hals, opened its doors. It had been an exceedingly happy thought to make a museum of this sedate, stylish building, erected by Lieven de Key in 1608. No building in Haarlem had retained to the same extent the dignity of the seventeenth century. The grand scale of the inner court guaranteed the necessary peace and moreover ensured good light in the rooms. One problem was however to arise eventually: the steady growth of the collections once again resulted in shortage of space, which could only be partially overcome.

AFTER THE SECOND WORLD WAR

After the Second World War the Dutch museums continued to develop in the direction they had taken in the first quarter of the twentieth century but at a quicker pace. The splendid work of the Foundation for the recovery of Netherlands artistic property has been of the greatest importance. During the war the Netherlands Government in London had consulted with those of other countries which were occupied by the Germans, on the measures to be taken in respect to the works of art looted by the occupying power. As far as the Netherlands were concerned, the point was not so much that works of art had been taken from museums as that many private possessions had been removed across the frontiers and that the total national estate had been seriously impoverished. In order to remedy this state of affairs, an authority was created which, in close collaboration with the allied armies, managed after Germany's capitulation to return a considerable quantity of the looted property. Part of this has come to the State of the Netherlands. The Foundation for the recovery of Netherlands artistic property, which administered this enormous stock of art works, made long-term loans to Dutch museums of those works which were important enough to qualify for such treatment.

The Rijksmuseum in particular benefited from this in all its sections. The collection of paintings was enriched by no fewer than forty-eight items. Among them were two works by Rembrandt: the great *Dead Peacocks* (p. 290) and the little portrait of the Spanish-Jewish physician *Ephraïm Bueno*. There were also Jan Steen's *Sacrifice of Iphigenia;* a sober still-life by Jan van de Velde; the *Portrait of Jacob de Graeff* by Gerard ter Borch; landscapes by Jacob van Geel, Bartholomeus Breenbergh, Jan van der Heyden and the impressive portrait of Burgomaster Ernst van Beveren by Aert de Gelder. Moreover many Italian paintings, mainly from the former collections of Dr F. Mannheimer and Professor Otto Lanz, both of Amsterdam, were also acquired. Thus an unexpected crop of great beauty was harvested by the museum after the war.

After this highly welcome increase the aim during the post-war years was to fill gaps in the collections before the soaring market should be completely exhausted. These existed primarily among the Northern-Netherlandish 'Primitives', the early Renaissance and Mannerist Dutch painters. Secondly, the national school of the eighteenth century qualified for expansion. Also the representation of foreign painters was, in many ways, still weak. And as regards the seventeenth-century Dutch painting, rich though it was, some things yet remained to be acquired. There was Rembrandt's work, which was still less well represented in Amsterdam than in museums abroad, such as the Hermitage at Leningrad, the National Gallery in Washington, the Metropolitan Museum in New York, or the National Gallery in London – and this despite Schmidt Degener's zeal and the pieces lent by the Foundation for the recovery of Netherlands artistic property. The collection of history paintings showed some gaps.

Through the increase in the grants for purchases, the help of the Commission for the Sale of Photographs, the Jubilee Fund of 1958, liberal donations and legacies and the never-failing support of the Rembrandt Society, various opportunities for acquiring important paintings did occur. The richest increases were among North-Netherlands 'Primitives' and Renaissance painters, with works by the Master of the Virgo inter Virgines, Geertgen tot Sint Jans, Jacob Cornelisz van Oostsanen, Mostaert, Scorel, Maerten van Heemskerck, Lucas van Leyden, Dirck Jacobsz and Pieter Pietersz. The collection of seventeenth-century Dutch painters was expanded with the exceedingly fine *Adoration of the Shepherds* (p. 288) by Jan Steen, one of the rare religious subjects by this master, two still-lifes by Abraham van Beyeren, the large *Interior of the Portuguese Synagogue* (p. 181) by Emanuel de Witte and a canvas by Hendrick Terbrugghen. To Rembrandt's work in the Rijksmuseum were added the captivating sketch of Joseph recounting his dreams painted in grey (see p. 290; bought in 1946, thanks to co-operation between the Rembrandt Society and the Commission for the Sale of Photographs); a *Self-portrait* by the master (loaned in 1950); a youthful work *Old Tobias* (loan 1956); a late portrait of his son Titus (loan from the Louvre, 1956) and, on the occasion of the 150th anniversary of the museum in 1958, an early, *Laughing Self-Portrait* (p. 189). I do not propose to specify the acquisitions in the field of eighteenth-century and foreign art which have been obtained since 1945, nor the paintings of an historical nature.

The Mauritshuis no less than the Rijksmuseum was enriched by the activities of the Foundation for the recovery of Netherlands artistic property. Through its activities twenty paintings came to increase the collection in 1948. But this acquisition was greatly exceeded by the generous legacy of the former Director, Dr A. Bredius, who died in 1946. In his will he had laid down that the twenty-five paintings which he had loaned to the Mauritshuis during his lifetime were to be made over to it for good. This meant that a collection of Rembrandts such as was not to be found anywhere else in the world would stay in the museum for ever: the great *Saul and David* (p. 195), *The Negroes* (p. 291), the portraits of Rembrandt's mother and of his father; the *Homer* (p. 291); the *Minerva* and the *Andromeda*. The collection also included works by Ambrosius Benson, Abraham van Beyeren, Brekelenkam, Calraet, Chardin, Aelbert Cuyp, Carel and Barend Fabritius, Hendrick Pot, Salomon van Ruysdael, Jan Steen, Jan van Goyen, Willem van de Velde the Younger and Moreelse, each of them highly important specimens of their particular style.

The following year a long cherished wish came to fulfilment: Mr and Mrs Ten Cate donated a badly needed painting by Pieter de Hooch representing a courtyard behind a house in Delft. Fine works by Rubens, Jacob Jordaens, Frans Hals and Bartholomeus Breenberg (p. 167) have been purchased in recent years and, finest of all Rembrandt's *Last Self-portrait* (p. 291) (purchased in 1947 with the support of the Rembrandt Society and many private donors).

The story of the Boymans Museum's fortunes since 1945 begins exactly like those of the Rijksmuseum and the Mauritshuis: here too, was a unique increase thanks to the Foundation for the recovery of Netherlands artistic property. Twenty-four paintings from the former Koenigs collection came to the Museum in this way. Among them were nine sketches in oil by Rubens and works by Cornelis Engebrechtsz, Patinir, Van der Neer, Avercamp, Jan Steen, De Witte, Van Dyck and Jordaens.

In 1939, to stimulate purchases for the museum, the Boymans Museum Foundation was established. It has made possible the purchase of many works – not only in the field of paintings; for instance, in 1940 four sketches by Rubens, already mentioned, from the estate of Franz Koenigs who had died in that year. Other institutions such as the Erasmus Foundation also helped the museum to purchase works of art, which now cost ever larger sums of money.

It would be impracticable enumerate the names of all those who, in the past two generations, have helped through donations and legacies to make the collections of the Boymans Museum of international importance. The long line of Rotterdam benefactors culminated – and, for the time being, ended – with a world-famous collector who rivalled the greatest Dutch collectors of all times, if indeed he did not surpass them, Daniël George van Beuningen (1877–1955). The undisputed highlight of his collection was Van Eyck's *Three Marys at the Sepulchre* (p. 81), bought from the Cook Collection at Richmond. No less important was *The Great Tower of Babel* (p. 120–1) by Pieter Brueghel. Van Beuningen moreover possessed a very rare, early triptych from Liège (p. 273), works by Dirck Bouts, Memlinc, Gerard David and Stephan Lochner, Provoost, Van Orley, the Master of Saint Gilles and the Master of the Life of Mary, an altar-wing by the Master of Aix, the miniature-like panel with the *Glorification of the Virgin* (p. 274, where it is titled 'Virgin in Majesty') by Geertgen tot Sint Jans, only discovered after the war, a Gossaert (p. 109), a *Holy Family* (p. 277) by Dürer, an important collection of Dutch paintings from the seventeenth century, interesting Italian pieces, and, from the eighteenth century, works by Watteau (p. 302), Chardin (p. 261), Hubert Robert (p. 302) and Guardi (p. 301). We pass by the nineteenth-century part of the collection, the Italian bronzes, the drawings and applied art. With its acquisition of this enormous purchase in 1958, the Boymans Museum definitely became one of the world's great museums.

In 1949 the Van Beuningen Collection had been shown at the traditional Summer Exhibition at the Boymans Museum. It was a festive occasion in commemoration of the centenary of the museum. The 'proud possessor' of all these fine works could not then foresee that the Rotterdam municipality, out of gratitude for Van Beuningen, would seven years later add his name to that of the founder of the Museum. Seen in retrospect, the 1949 Summer Exhibition acquires a symbolic meaning: Boymans and Van Beuningen together characterise a century of Rotterdam art life.

The Frans Hals Museum too received its share of works distributed by the Foundation for the recovery of Netherlands artistic property. Apart from fine seventeenth-century pieces such as a family group by Jan Miense Molenaar (p. 155), the sixteenth-century (unfinished) *Discovery of America* (p. 275) by Jan Mostaert is worthy of note. The purchasing policy which had been followed in the past has continued unchanged in recent times. An important addition to the collections was a colourful *Dance round the Golden Calf* (p. 128) by Carel van Mander which was bought in 1952.

The picture which we have given here of the history of the four most important Dutch museums of old paintings cannot, for lack of space, be complete. It is, moreover, one-sided, for the limits of this book compel us to leave undiscussed the collecting of nineteenth- and twentieth-century paintings. We have also had to leave out the history of the collecting of all other kinds of art objects. And even this would not be complete without a sketch of the fortunes of auctioneering and the art-trade which has made collecting possible. There is also the important function of the loan exhibition; more and more the scope and frequency is expanded, especially in modern times, and often splendid results are achieved. And it would be interesting to enquire into the statistics of visits to museums and temporary exhibitions. All of this, taken together, would form a deeply enthralling fragment of cultural history. But even the restricted field we have covered reveals a reflexion of the national past of the Netherlands, the views, taste and spheres of interest of the Dutch people through the ages. And not of them alone: it is also a mirror of the generation which lived just before us and of the one to which we ourselves belong.

JAN VAN EYCK (ca. 1385/90–1441)
possibly with his brother Hubert (ca. 1370–1426)
THE THREE MARIES AT THE SEPULCHRE   Panel
Boymans-van Beuningen Museum   Height 71.5 cm. (28″)
                                                       Width 89   cm. (33″)

The painter has depicted most impressively the discovery of the Resurrection, as if it had taken place in the Middle Ages, by piecing together the
information given in the Gospels. The miracle takes place in a paradisiac
landscape, recalling that of the centre panel of the *Adoration of the Lamb*
at Ghent. Following an old tradition already found in the work of early
Italian primitives such as Duccio, the three Maries approach from the left,
each dressed in a distinctive colour, but united as a group by the milk-white
of the headdresses they wear. On the right are three sleeping soldiers who
form a diagonal line running from the foreground to the middle-ground of
the picture. The drawing of these sturdily built figures contrasts sharply
with the fluid outlines of the Maries.

In the background Jerusalem's many towers give strong vertical accents
to the composition. Although the view of the city is imaginary, the Mosque
of Omar can be recognised.

In the centre, surrounded by these different elements, stands Christ's
empty grave. This is a classical sarcophagus seen in reversed perspective,
and not a tomb cut from the rock as in the Bible. On its long lid, placed
across the tomb, is seated an angel with waving gold hair, dressed entirely
in white. This figure is smaller, and quite different in appearance from the
Maries and the soldiers, clearly making a contrast between the heavenly
and earthly figures. In depicting only one angel St Mark's Gospel (16:5) is
followed (St Luke 29:4 and St John 20:12 speak of *two* angels in white).
The rocks at the left are later additions and did not originally complete
the composition on this side. Another later addition, made about 1470,
is the coat of arms of the chronicler Philippe de Commines in the bottom
right-hand corner. Above this can be seen the ends of a few slanting golden
rays which formed part of a halo which appeared in another panel, originally placed to the right of the painting. This has been lost, but it may be
assumed that it represented the Resurrection of Christ. The scene of the
Three Maries at the Sepulchre was either the centre panel of a triptych,
or part of a polyptych making a series like a frieze.

The attribution of the panel presents a difficult problem. On stylistic
grounds and because of the incredibly high quality of the work, it is often
included among the early works of Jan van Eyck. Some authorities,

however, including Panofsky, suggest the possibility of a collaboration between Jan and his elder brother Hubert. It may have been painted about 1420. It is, in any case, older than the altarpiece at Ghent, which was begun before 1426, the year of Hubert's death.

About 1470 the work was owned by Philippe de Commines. It is not mentioned again until 4th May 1770, when it was in the sale of J. Wynckel-man, Lord of the Neetersche at Bruges. After this it appeared at Bernhard Bauwen's sale (8th August 1826), W. Middleton in Brussels, at Christie's (26th January 1872, no. 140); the collection of Sir Charles Robinson; the collection of Sir Francis Cook, Sir Frederick Cook, and Sir Herbert Cook, Richmond. In 1939 it passed into the collections of D. G. van Beuningen, Vierhouten, Holland, and was acquired from his estate in 1958 by the Boymans-van Beuningen Museum.

A DORDRECHT MASTER (ca. 1450–1460)

Sᴛ Aɢɴᴇs ᴡɪᴛʜ Gᴇᴇʀᴛʀᴜʏ ᴠᴀɴ Sʟɪɴɢᴇʟᴀɴᴅᴛ   Panel

Rijksmuseum No. 131 H 1   Height 60.5 cm. (23³/₄″)

Width 46.5 cm. (18¹/₄″)

This panel is one of the earliest surviving examples of Northern-Nether-landish painting. The discovery of this work was something of a sensation. In 1957 it appeared on the English art market, as Flemish, but doubts arose about this attribution. Heraldry pointed the way to its proper indenti-fication. The coat of arms above the head of the female donor belongs to the Haeck and Van Slingelandt van der Tempel families. Adriaen Haeck came from a Dordrecht family. Between 1436 and 1448 his name appears several times as sheriff, treasurer and burgomaster of his native town. He died, presumably, in 1448 or shortly afterwards, apparently without leaving any children. His wife, Geertruy van Slingelandt, belonged to an aristo-cratic family. We do not know the exact dates of her life but from the painting it appears that she must have survived her husband, for it can be seen from her clothes that she was a widow.

At Dordrecht there existed in the fifteenth century a Convent dedicated to St Agnes. Among its female residents between 1450 and 1477 there were no fewer than four relatives of Geertruy Haeck-van Slingelandt. The panel in the Rijksmuseum shows us that Geertruy herself must also have been interested in the St Agnes Convent. Did she perhaps have the picture made for the convent, when she was a widow?

It may be assumed that the work was painted by a Dordrecht artist. The alternative would be a painter from a nearby town or a travelling artist but in view of its style the latter appears less likely, as the style is far from advanced for the middle of the fifteenth century. The panel would appear to have been the work of a man who, in a somewhat secluded place, con-tinued older traditions which had been replaced in more important centres by newer concepts.

For a long time the painting was privately owned in Britain. On 17th May 1957 it was auctioned in London (as by a painter of the Bruges school). In 1958 the Rijksmuseum acquired the panel from a British art dealer.

MASTER OF THE GATHERING OF THE MANNA (ca. 1470)

THE OFFERING BY THE JEWS   Panel

Boymans-van Beuningen Museum No. 272 b   Height 69.5 cm. (27¹/₄″)

Width 51.5 cm. (20¹/₄″)

This anonymous artist derives his name from a panel in the Boymans-van Beuningen Museum which is the pendant of the painting reproduced here. He was one of the 'small masters' of the Northern-Netherlandish primitive and was only discovered a few years ago. From the style of his work it may be surmised that he lived about 1470. It has been suggested that he may have worked in Haarlem but, failing material for comparison, this remains a shot in the dark.

What strikes us first in the art of this anonymous painter, is the vivid colouring. Fiery red, strong yellow and olive green – he has the courage to put them beside one another, against a background of delicately chosen grey in all kinds of shades. His white is clear, with soft, light blue shades. He avoids the use of black as much as possible so that his palette never becomes heavy. A second characteristic of his style is a fortunate feeling for composition. He chooses a high view-point and is consequently in a position to show much without indistinctness or giving an impression of untidiness. Everything on the panel can easily be seen, for the small groups are logically composed, and together form a circle, which effectively suggests space. The curve of the circle is accentuated by the slanting of the choir of the temple building where the action takes place – the holocaust of the Jews (Leviticus 1 and 6), which in the Middle Ages passed as an Old-Testament parallel of the Last Supper.

The figures have something angular about them and are slightly stylised, but their faces and gestures are distinct. They are concentrating intently on their actions. Nowhere in this work is there any pretence or idle ostentation. It is honest and, to a certain extent, uncomplicated. Its simplicity is undisturbed by archaeological or other details, by showy learning, by nervousness in the elaboration of the theme or by tension. All the qualities mentioned are typical of the spirit of the Northern-Netherlandish art of painting. May I go so far as to call this little painting representative of the 'Dutch bourgeoisie'?

The panel probably formed part of an altarpiece composed of many small scenes. It comes from the collection of the Earl of Mount Edgcombe and was in 1951 acquired by the Boymans-van Beuningen Museum on the art market.

84

GEERTGEN TOT SINT JANS (1460/1465–1490/1495 ?)
THE ADORATION OF THE MAGI   Panel
Rijksmuseum No. 950 A 1   Height 90 cm. (35³/₈″)
                                                Width 70 cm. (27⁵/₈″)

The praise of Geertgen tot Sint Jans was sung for the first time by his
Haarlem fellow-townsman Carel van Mander in his well known *Book of
Painters* which appeared in 1604. The facts given there are still the basis
for any life of the artist, about whom little is known. He was probably
born at Leyden and when young is supposed to have become a pupil of
Albert van Ouwater who was a famous painter in Haarlem at that time.
Geertgen's talent appears to have developed rapidly and before long he had
become the leader of the Haarlem School. He died when he was about
twenty-eight but despite his short life his art had considerable influence.
During the Reformation Geertgen's work became scattered and his name
was forgotten.

.Since 1808 the Rijksmuseum had owned a panel by Geertgen representing
The Holy Virgin in the Van der Pot Collection, which had been bought
in its entirety. At that time, however, the painting had not yet been
recognised as a work of the forgotten artist and was taken to be by
Hubert and Jan van Eyck. Only in consequence of the renewed interest in
the 'Primitives' was another work by the master acquired by the Rijksmuseum in 1904, the painting reproduced opposite. *The Adoration of the
Magi* conforms to tradition in the late Middle Ages. On the left appear the
three kings fantastically attired. The figure of the negro is simply a
blackened white man without any characteristic feature of the negro race,
of whose existence the painter evidently knew only from hearsay.

On the right, behind Mary with the Child and Joseph, is the stable with
the ox and the ass, vaguely reminiscent of a fragment of a Romanesque
church. Romanesque in this period should be interpreted both as 'Roman'
and as an indication of the approaching Renaissance. Through a mountain
landscape the Kings approach once again in the distance, each with his own
suite of handsomely attired horsemen. Again we see the artist's imagination
at work. He had apparently not seen mountains with his own eyes, any
more than negroes. But in front of this invented landscape we see a stream
with flowering bulrushes, both true to life and commonplace. This sort of
thing Geertgen had definitely seen himself, somewhere at the edge of a ditch
or in the Dutch dunes which were still swamps at that time. The painting
was bought in 1904 by the Rijksmuseum at the sale of W. Hekking, Jr.

ROGIER VAN DER WEYDEN
(ca. 1400–1464)
THE DESCENT FROM THE CROSS   Panel
Mauritshuis No. 264
Height 78 cm. (30³/₄")
Width 129 cm. (50³/₄")

The theme of *The Descent from the Cross*
was treated by Rogier van der Weyden
first in the magisterial altarpiece from
the Escorial which since 1939 has hung
in the Prado at Madrid, and is recognised
as his masterpiece. When later, about
1460, he again depicts the same subject
in a smaller picture, the artist's ideas
have changed considerably. The composition is less monumental, as is already
implied by the size; the figures are less
violent in their movements, their drawing is less tense and they look more as
though they were painted sculpture.
Their number has been increased by
one – the donor – but a different arrangement of the figures makes the crowd in
the scene at the Mauritshuis appear more
numerous than in Madrid. In the background the onlooker now perceives a
gentle Southern-Netherlandish landscape, whereas on the panel in the Prado
the event takes place in front of an even
golden background. Here the painter is
animated by a kinder and gentler spirit.
The picture is less dramatically moving but shows greater control and depth
of feeling. It is typical of the changes which had transformed spiritual life
in Flanders. The next generation is already making its presence felt. For
this reason the painting even used to be attributed to Memlinc.

Behind the donor, whose identity is uncertain, stand Saints Peter and
Paul. They are there as patron saints but do not take part in the drama

enacted before their eyes. They look as though they do not see it at all.
St Peter has his head slightly inclined towards his protegé, St Paul looks
rather vacantly before him. According to Dr A. B. de Vries they were
painted by a different hand.

About the origin of the painting nothing is known. In 1827 King
William I bought it from Baron de Keversberg, for the Mauritshuis.

MASTER OF THE VIRGO INTER VIRGINES
(probably active about 1470–1500)

MARY WITH CHILD SURROUNDED BY FOUR FEMALE SAINTS

(the 'Virgo inter Virgines')   Panel
Rijksmuseum No. 1538 VI   Height 123 cm. (48³/₄")
                                 Width 102 cm. (40¹/₈")

Art historians have been able to localise the anonymous painter known as
'Master of the Virgo inter Virgines' to Delft. He must have been one of
the most important Dutch artists of his time and have exerted much
influence. Characteristic of his style are the lean body-shapes of his figures
with pale, lank fingers, and the high, bulging foreheads of the women. His
colouring is delicate, with its tender pink-red and warm grey. He showed
restraint even in the portraying of jewels and precious materials which he
despised no more than his Flemish fellow-painters. He rarely allowed himself to be seduced into displaying that heavy splendour to which many of
the Flemish 'Primitives' gave free rein. In contrast with them, he always
retained a certain measure of reserve; it belonged to his strong feeling for
intimacy which, even in wide landscapes and panoramas, does not leave
him. How modestly Mary sits there in the almshouse, surrounded by four
saints, Cecily, Barbara, Ursula (she was the patron saint of Cologne and,
in Holland, of Delft) and Katharine. On the right in the background stand
two more female saints, Margaret with the dragon and, presumably, Mary
Magdalen with her ointment pot. On the other side the youthful John the
Evangelist and Jacob (?) are involved in a discussion. A scene with so
many female saints would appear to have been painted for a convent. There
are no documents giving us any information as to the origin of the
painting but when in 1808 it was transferred from the National Museum at
The Hague where it had hung since 1801, to the Royal Museum at Amsterdam, it was described as 'a convent altarpiece'. How the panel had come
to the National Museum is not clear. We know, however, that the grounds
and the archives of the Koningsveld Convent near Delft had, after its
secularisation in the sixteenth century, come to the State. Does the altar
piece also originate from this convent, perhaps, and was it kept by the
keeper of the archives at The Hague until the organisers of the new museum
brought it to light again in 1800? The title used in 1808 might well contain
the correct indication of its origin.

HANS MEMLINC (ca. 1433–1494)

PORTRAIT OF A MAN   Panel

Mauritshuis No. 595   Height 30.1 cm. (11³/₄″)

Width 22.3 cm.   (8³/₄″)

Although the back of the panel shows a family coat of arms, it has not yet been possible to decide who is the subject of the *Portrait of a Man* by Memlinc in the Mauritshuis. He was presumably one of the wealthy merchants of Bruges, the town where the painter worked throughout his life. The panel is likely to have been originally a wing of a diptych. On the other (the left) wing, a saint or the Madonna may have been portrayed, as in the case of the well-known little altarpiece with a portrait of Martin van Nieuwenhove in the St Ursula Hospital at Bruges. Memlinc was as much a painter of religious scenes as a portrait painter. In many of his altarpieces he inserted realistically-observed donors' portraits; in addition more than twenty-five independent portraits by him have survived. Of these the one at The Hague is among the most important. The head with luxuriant curly hair, and the broad shoulders which look even heavier owing to the fur-lined tabard, almost fill the whole picture, but the artist spared just enough room to indicate that his figure has been placed in space. Two small fragments of landscape, no more than minute triangles with some greenery, a church with a little tower, a few houses and some trees, above that a high, thinly clouded sky, suffice for him to suggest the whole breadth of the flat Flemish countryside. The problem of its distance from the portrayed figure, does not arise, as the man's shoulders hide the intermediate planes completely from the eye. Thus the landscape remains far in the distance and does not in any way draw the attention away from the head. But the artist has given his complete attention to this subsidiary matter and elaborated it with a fine brush, as though it were a miniature.

The painting appeared on 7th July 1894 at the sale of Sir Andrew Fontaine in London (catalogue no. 46) and was then described as a work of Antonello da Messina. On that occasion it was bought by the Rembrandt Society for the Mauritshuis.

HIERONYMUS BOSCH (probably about 1450–1516)

St Christopher and the Infant Jesus Panel

Boymans-van Beuningen Museum No. 50 d Height 113 cm. (44¹/₂″)

Width 71.5 cm. (28¹/₄″)

In the *Golden Legend,* Jacobus de Voragine (Chapter XCIX) describes the story of the giant Reprobus from Canaan who, looking for the most powerful master in the world, successively served the king of his country and the devil, after which a hermit at last pointed out to him the omnipotence of Jesus Christ. His profession was taking people on his broad shoulders across the river at a spot where there was no bridge. But once he almost succumbed under the seemingly easy task of carrying a child across. It was the Child Christ who bore the burden of the world. From this event the giant derived the name Christopher: bearer of Christ. In the Roman Catholic Church he became the patron of travellers.

The globe which Christ generally holds in his hand in portraits of Saint Christopher is absent in Hieronymus Bosch's painting, but apart from this it corresponds to the usual iconography, with a few additions here and there that are typical of the painter's interest in all kinds of picturesque, demoniac and piquant details. For instance, he included the hermit of the story looking out of a strange pitcher hung up from an arid tree in which he lives. The devil also appears on the panel in the shape of a dragon who sticks out his head above the wall of a distant fortress situated on water, thus terrifying a bather. Bosch portrayed this story with his characteristic imagination, exquisite colours and with delicate refinement. The strawberry-red cloak of the saint as well as that of the Child Christ are blown by the wind and, with a wide sweep fill a large part of the panel. They make the giant seem big and dominating in the wide, elaborated miniature landscape with the river in shades varying from greenish to grey-blue and the far, deep-blue distance.

The painting is known to have been in Italy and later in the collection of F. Koenigs at Haarlem. In 1940 it was donated by D. G. van Beuningen to the Boymans Museum Foundation.

HIERONYMUS BOSCH (probably about 1450–1516)
THE VAGABOND   Panel, round
Boymans-van Beuningen Museum No. 51   Diameter 70.50 cm. (27³/₄")

This painting used to be called *The Prodigal Son,* having been interpreted as such by Gustav Glück in 1904. The figure of the lean, unshaven vagrant dressed in rags and the house on the left, in the door of which a couple is courting while a woman ogles from the window, gave rise to this interpretation. Later, however, objections arose to this biblical title. The portrayal of the man appeared to depart too much from the customary iconography of the Prodigal Son. For that reason preference was given to the more general term *The Vagabond.* All the same it is likely to have had a special meaning, probably a pessimistic moral. Some critics have even gone further and looked for an allegory on human life in general.

The more we know of Bosch's work (and our knowledge has been much increased in recent years), the more allusions and symbols it seems to contain. Such allusions have been found in *The Vagabond.* The two figures in the doorway of the inn at which the sign of the swan hangs, may represent the constellation of Gemini (the Twins), the indecent little man by the corner of the house, Aquarius (the Waterman). *The Vagabond* himself may be a man born under the constellation of Saturn who as a result is receiving his part of the sorrow caused on earth by this planet. Lotte Brand Philip has perceptively suggested that this circular panel may have been one of four on the outside of an altar piece, representing the four elements and the four temperaments; the three others must have been lost but we can reconstruct what they looked like from old replicas. At this period the vagabond was often used as a symbol for the Earth and at the same time for melancholy. Finally it is not out of the question that the melancholy exile, the Prodigal Son, the lonely wanderer is a self-portrait of the painter.

These different interpretations do not necessarily contradict one another, for the iconography of late-medieval art was an elaborate system in which a single figure can be variously interpreted. Bosch understood the secret of bringing together many intricate intellectual themes in subtly painted scenes – pointed, sensitive and full of atmosphere, in which complete harmony was achieved between the sublime manner of painting and the complicated subjects.

The painting was successively in the collections of T. Schiff and Dr A. Figdor, both in Vienna. In 1932 it was acquired by the Rotterdam Museum with the help of the legacy of J. P. van der Schilden, the Rembrandt Society and friends of the Museum.

QUENTIN MATSYS (1465 or 1466–1530)
MADONNA IN A LANDSCAPE   Panel
Boymans-van Beuningen Museum   Height 41 cm. (16^1/$_8$″)
                                                 Width 28 cm. (11″)

'Whoever has familiarised himself with the world of Quentin, feels elevated, as though he had taken flight from the brown earth in a glass bowl.' With these poetical words Dr Max J. Friedländer begins his interpretation of Master Quentin's personality in his famous series of volumes on early Dutch painting. He then describes the charming and noble female figures in Quentin's work, and the precociously mature children. He dwells on the fact that the artist used round, smooth and supple shapes instead of angular ones and that he revelled in the ceaseless melody of undulating and continuous lines, but also that, despite all the period's new possibilities, he remained linked with older Dutch art both in his compositions and in his painting technique. Matsys lived at a time of transition between the Gothic world and the Renaissance. In the eyes of posterity this transition often assumes the shape of a sharp division, of an irreconcilable conflict. Many contemporaries however, cannot have felt this so clearly. They saw the possibility of synthesis. The Antwerp painter Quentin Matsys, in particular, understood it. His tender *Madonna in a Landscape* in the Boymans-van Beuningen Museum reveals his understanding in unparalleled fashion, and is one of his most completely successful works.

Before Mr D. G. van Beuningen acquired it, the painting was privately owned in Paris. With the core of his collection it came in 1958 to the Rotterdam Museum.

VITTORE CRIVELLI
(active between 1481 and 1501)
St Bonaventura   Panel
Rijksmuseum No. 737 E 2
Height 125 cm. (49¹/₄″)
Width   40 cm. (15³/₄″)

The high, narrow panels with holy figures
by Carlo and Vittore Crivelli are in all
probability parts of altar pieces which were
once in Venetian churches. Such retables are
similar in appearance to the iconostases of
Greek Orthodox churches decorated with
stately rows of saints standing in front of
an even background of gold. Of all Italian
towns, Venice was situated nearest to and
had always had most contacts with the
Byzantine Empire.

But the manner in which the Crivelli
brothers painted these figures was Italian.
They lived during the transition from Gothic
to the Renaissance. The luxuriant, blond
hair of Mary Magdalen is almost like a
German Gothic sculpture, hard of drawing
and calligraphically curled. Also Gothic are
the tendril motifs and the leaves on the
gold-coloured bodice of the saint and the
moulded edges of her cuffs, as well as the
angular folds in which her cloak hangs
down. But the grey stone plinth with
cherubs' heads on which she stands and the
garlands of flowers behind her head are
pure Renaissance style.

St Bonaventura shows, less strongly, a
mixture of the two styles. The points of the

(ca. 1430/1435–ca. 1495)
Sᴛ Mᴀʀʏ Mᴀɢᴅᴀʟᴇɴ Panel
Rijksmuseum No. 737 D 1
Height 152 cm. (59⁷/₈″)
Width 49 cm. (19¹/₄″)

halo behind his head, the folds of his cowl
and the canopies above the embroidered
figures of saints on the brim of his cope are
reminiscent of Gothic, but these figures
themselves and the round arcs of the niches
in which they stand, as also the cherubs,
belong to the Renaissance. Working in a
centre where all these different streams met,
the Crivellis knew how to create unity out
of diversity and bring harmony to it.

The panel of *Mary Magdalen* which must
have been painted about 1475, left Venice
at a time unknown to us and from the Solly
Collection went to the Kaiser Friedrich
Museum in Berlin. Later the panel was
bought by Dr F. Mannheimer of Amster-
dam whose collection after the second World
War came to the Dutch nation. Lent by the
Dienst voor's Rijks Kunstvoorwerpen to the
Rijksmuseum since 1949.

St Bonaventura with its pendant representing *St Louis* of France, formed part of
the C. Butler Collection, of Warren Wood,
Hatfield, before being sold in London. It
was bought by J. W. Edwin vom Rath of
Amsterdam and bequeathed by him to the
Rijksmuseum in 1941.

PIERO DI LORENZO called *DI COSIMO* (1462–1521)
PORTRAIT OF FRANCESCO GIAMBERTI   Panel
Rijksmuseum No. 1875 B 1   Height 47   cm. (18½″)
                                       Width 35.5 cm. (13¾″)

Francesco Giamberti (1405–1480) exercised the profession of furniture maker and intarsia worker at Florence. He was the founder of the famous family of architects and sculptors bearing the name of Sangallo. This work has a companion portrait of his son, the great architect Giuliano da Sangallo (1445–1516).

Like the two sitters, the painter Piero di Cosimo was a Florentine. He was born in 1462. In 1480, when Francesco Giamberti died, he was therefore only about eighteen years of age, whereas Giuliano da Sangallo was then about thirty-seven. In view of the age of the latter in his portrait and because of the style of painting, the date of the two paintings of father and son is usually put at about 1505; this means that the portrait of Francesco Giamberti must be posthumous. The son probably ordered the two portraits as a proud memento for posterity of himself but at the same time as a token of respectful homage to the memory of his father to whom he undoubtedly owed a lot. Did Giuliano's removal from Florence to Rome at the end of 1505 perhaps occasion the commissioning of the panels?

In order to give Francesco Giamberti's head a good likeness, Piero di Cosimo probably worked after a medal cast during the lifetime of the sitter. This might explain why he rendered the head in such sharp profile in contrast to that of his son who is seen in three-quarter-face. In the background is a sunny landscape. It has been very carefully treated in a technique reminiscent of the Flemish painters of that period and a little earlier – among others of artists like Hans Memlinc. Perhaps his paintings were by then already known in Italy.

The Florentine painter and writer Vasari saw the portraits of Francesco and Giuliano in the middle of the sixteenth century. He copied the painting of the son to illustrate his book on great painters, sculptors and architects. Both paintings were owned by Francesco da Sangallo (1494–1576), son of Giuliano and therefore the grandson and namesake of Francesco Giamberti. Later they were the property of Prince William III of Orange. With his estate they went to the Friesian branch of the House of Nassau. King William I gave them to the Mauritshuis, which in 1948 lent them to the Rijksmuseum.

LUCAS VAN LEYDEN (possibly 1489–1533)
THE DANCE OF THE ISRAELITES
ROUND THE GOLDEN CALF   Panel
Rijksmuseum No. 1452 A 2
                centre piece Height 93 cm. (36⁵/₈")
                            Width 67 cm. (28³/₈")
                wings each Height 91 cm. (35⁷/₈")
                            Width 30 cm. (11³/₄")

In the *Great Book of Painters* which came out in
1604, Carel van Mander relates how he had seen
'very excellent and special work by Lucas at
Amsterdam in the Calverstraet' in which the
Dance round the Golden Calf hat been represented.
'In this feast', he says, 'one sees very vividly
displayed the wanton nature of the people and
their unchaste lust revealing them completely as
they are.' This piece was rediscovered in private
ownership in Paris in 1953; in the same year it
was bought by the Rijksmuseum.

   Even without this mention by Van Mander, it
would not have been difficult to recognise this
colourful triptych as a most important work by
one of Holland's greatest Renaissance artists. He
may have painted it about 1525. The foreground
is completely filled with the motley bustle of the
feasting Israelites. The half-figures of two children
in the centre talking to one another remind one
momentarily of the well-known angels beneath
Raphael's Sistine Madonna, in a more 'bourgeois',
Dutch form. The subject proper only comes on
the second plane, where small and decorative figures dance exuberantly
round the golden idol. And even smaller, almost lost and hardly noticeable
in the grand mountain range, after much searching the onlooker finds Moses.
He is seen once high on a mountain top, kneeling in a dense cloud, and a
second time, accompanied by Joshua, as during his descent he lifts the
Tables of the Law in anger to hurl them at the calf (Exodus 24:15–18 and
32:11–19). The composition, the details and the handling of paint are
picturesque and brilliantly expressive, but there is no religious feeling.
While the figure of Moses is small and inconspicuous by contrast those of

the feasting Jews are prominent. For a piece of devotion it is really a shocking performance. Whoever sees this, begins to understand why Iconoclasm was a historic necessity.

We do not know the name of the owner of the painting, who lived in Amsterdam about 1600. In 1671 the triptych was owned by Jacob Wuytiers in Amsterdam. He bequeathed it to his son Dirck in 1679. Later it was sold at the sale of Jacob Cromhout and Jasper Loskart (Amsterdam, 7th–8th May 1709) and once again in the sale of the Marquis du Blaisel (Paris, 16th March 1870). Thereafter it belonged to Mme Bigniez in Paris.

AERTGEN VAN LEYDEN (1498–1564)
THE RAISING OF LAZARUS

Rijksmuseum No. 1449 D 1

Panel

Height 75.5 cm. (29³/₄″)
Width 78.5 cm. (30⁷/₈″)

Aertgen van Leyden is a little-known artist. Van Mander gave a description of his life in 1604, but thereafter he was forgotten. Only in 1939 Professor J. Q. van Regteren Altena succeeded in compiling a survey of his work. In 1946 the first painting by the master made its entry into the Rijksmuseum. In some foreign museums and private collections panels and drawings by his hand had, in the meantime, been recognised.

Aertgen was a Leyden man born and bred. He received his training there from Cornelis Engebrechtsz and stayed in the town of his birth until his death.

In the main Aertgen painted religious scenes but on to these he thrust the profane realism of the Renaissance concepts which in his time were working their way through into the Northern Netherlands. He liked compositions in three dimensions, effects of perspective, drawn-out figures whose long limbs stuck out in all directions moving violently, and unexpected combinations of gay colours. The source of these qualities can already be found in his teacher, but in Aertgen's work they have become more elaborate, more pregnant, more relaxed and also more capricious. This makes his art arresting.

In the panel of *The Raising of Lazarus* in the Rijksmuseum, most of the figures have been grouped, in a wonderful subtle manner, in a circle seen in perspective. On its extreme right Lazarus has been portrayed; the two men talking to one another are on the extreme left; Christ stands in the centre and on either side of him are the two sisters of the man risen from the dead, these three figures forming an arc of the circle. By this complicated composition a strong link between the various figures has been achieved; as a result they really stand right in the middle of the surrounding landscape. The very personal application of colour contributes to creating the result aimed at.

The painting was acquired in 1946 on the English art market.

106

JAN GOSSAERT VAN MABUSE (about 1475–about 1535)
The Metamorphosis of Hermaphrodite and Salmacis   Panel
Boymans-van Beuningen Museum   Height 32.8 cm. (13")
                                                Width 21.5 cm. (8½")

The Renaissance, which to an important extent arose as a result of renewed interest in the Classics, owed to this source its strongly literary character. For the present-day onlooker, usually less versed and less interested in the Greek and Roman stories, it is often difficult to understand what the fifteenth- and sixteenth-century artists felt when they applied their best artistic abilities to all those weird, often sensual, mythological tales.

Such considerations occur to the viewer of the painting of *The Metamorphosis of Hermaphrodite and Salmacis*. Ovid recounts in his *Metamorphoses* (IV, 285), how Salmacis, the nymph of a well, prayed to be allowed to become one with the man she loved, but who did not respond to her love. How this prayer was answered Jan Gossaert portrayed on a small panel, in delicate colours, painted thinly and glazed. The water of the well is of an amazing subtlety, the mood of the surrounding landscape is sunny. Of course, the two bodies have been very finely observed anatomically as the new ideas of the time required. Their white muscles give them the appearance of antique marble statues. Gossaert had been able to study such sculpture closely during a journey to Rome, undertaken in 1508–1509. The impressions formed were to remain with him all his life. The struggle between the two figures – the young man vainly attempting to escape the grip of the violent woman who loves him – has been rendered in a lively manner. On the left, in the background, one sees, very small, the process of unification in a later phase, when it is already half completed.

It is not known for whom this painting was made. Mr D. G. van Beuningen acquired it in the North of France. With the core of his collection it was bought in 1958 by the Boymans Museum.

JAN VAN SCOREL (1495–1562)

THE YOUNG SCHOLAR

Boymans-van Beuningen Museum No. 412

Panel

Height 46.5 cm. (18¹/₄″)
Width 35 cm. (13³/₄″)

It was during one of those fortunate periods of balance between aesthetic and intellectual, political and religious, spiritual and materialistic forces that Jan van Scorel painted his young pupil. It was 1531. The new ideas of the Renaissance had conquered but they had not yet become so commonplace as to degenerate into routine; the penetration of Humanism had a refreshing, civilising effect, but the religious struggle had not yet blazed up in all its sharpness and destructive violence; the old political balance and the traditional régime in town and country were still strong; trade and industry flourished, excessive pursuit of profit with its consequent train of intrigue and crises did not yet seriously disturb society. In that world Scorel had every reason to portray a fresh, quiet and clever young man. He is healthy in body and spirit. The vivid colouring of the panel corresponds to the liveliness of his face and hands. We see a boy without 'complexes', the painting is suitably direct in approach and has a simple, well-considered composition.

Scorel shows clearly that he is not only a painter but also a Humanist: the Latin texts which he put on the picture are not only there to indicate that the pupil is taught Classics but that the artist, too, had mastered them. The clear Roman lettering had only recently been taken over from the tombstones and temple inscriptions of the Ancients to replace the Gothic writing so difficult to read and operates here as handsome ornament. On top stand, very accurately, the year and age of the sitter: 1531 – AETATIS – 12. It is typical of the new period. The religious Middle Ages were not so interested in such details of human life. Underneath one reads the philosophical maxim: QUIS DIVES? QUI NIL CUPIT – QUIS PAUPER? AVAR (Who is rich? He who does not covet anything. Who poor? The miser). On the bit of paper which the child holds in his hand it has finally been written: 'Omnia dat dominus non habet ergo minus' ('The Lord gives everything and yet has no less'). With this the thoughts of the Humanist returned to his Creator.

The painting was bought by the Boymans Museum on 13th October 1864 at the sale of J. van der Hoop.

110

MAERTEN VAN HEEMSKERCK (1498–1574)

PORTRAIT OF ANNA CODDE

Rijksmuseum No. 1128 A 2

Panel

Height 84.5 cm. (33¹/₈″)
Width 65 cm. (25⁵/₈″)

It is, in my view, no exaggeration to say that Anna Codde is the sweetest woman ever to have been portrayed by a Dutch painter. When portrayed, in 1529, she was twenty-six years old. So much was related in an inscription cut in the original frame which still surrounds the panel. In 1522 she had married Master Pieter Bicker Gerritsz (1495–1567), Master of the Mint and later, after 1534, Sheriff of Amsterdam. The Bickers belonged to the ruling class.

The young woman is dressed with refined simplicity in only brown and black, a starched white hood on her head, exceedingly flattering to her rosy cheeks, and a fine white blouse decorated with little pearls. The face has something aristocratic but the painting remains 'bourgeois' nevertheless. This is not because of the spinning-wheel behind which Anna is working so zealously. We must remember that at the beginning of the sixteenth century the spinning-wheel was still something new, an instrument invented not long before which in the early years of its existence was often a precious piece of furniture, handsomely turned and sometimes colourfully inlaid. Working-class women were not yet using them at the time. The spinning-wheel therefore marked Mrs Bicker as a prosperous lady, though not a noblewoman, despite the fact that the wooden panel in the background has been decorated with a classical frame, a fashionable novelty the Renaissance had just introduced.

The spinning-wheel, moreover, serves as a foil to the figure and at the same time affords the painter the opportunity of showing his model's hands in an occupation and thus giving life to the scene. The thin white thread between the elegant fingers of the left hand is drawn with a very fine brush-stroke. It is an integral part of the airy play of lines which keeps the composition of the whole in such excellent harmony. The modest rust red of the decorated band around the knot of flax formed a desirable colour-accent to break the monotony.

The portrait came, probably by inheritance, from the Bickers, Huyberts, Ruytenburgh, Van Leyen and van Rhenen to the Schimmelpenninck van der Oye families at Voorst and in 1931, to Jonkheer R. E. W. van Weede at The Hague. In 1948 it was donated, together with its pendant, to the Rijksmuseum by Messrs D. and N. Katz.

HANS HOLBEIN THE YOUNGER (1497–1543)
PORTRAIT OF A MAN WITH A FALCON   Panel
Mauritshuis No. 277   Height 25 cm. (9⁷/₈″)
                                       Width 19 cm. (7¹/₂″)

England and English art owe an inestimable debt of gratitude to Hans
Holbein. When he left Basle to go to England where he entered the service
of Henry VIII as court painter, he presented his new fatherland with a
highly developed art of portraiture which England had previously lacked.
He created the state portrait and by doing so he founded a long-lived tradition.
For generations to come gifted portrait painters were drawn from the European
continent to England, as long as this country could not supply its own
needs. Holbein was only able to exercise that power by his startling abilities
as a painter. He painted many portraits of the English aristocracy in their
handsome clothes of wool, fur, velvet and silk, with their trappings of
costly decorations and sparkling jewels, looking quietly and often not a
little haughtily ahead of them. No doubt they were very pleased with this
court painter who always knew how to maintain the appropriate distance
and never made them appear insignificant or ugly but always at their best,
as a London society-photographer still knows how to do with his models.
It is Holbein's greatness that his art did not suffer under this working
procedure. He always maintained his thorough, noble, refined quality, and
a subtlety which was not weakened by routine. His working method was
really more that of a miniaturist than of a painter of more sizeable works
but the great line of his compositions has in no way suffered thereby.

From the inscription in the background it is evident that Holbein painted
the portrait reproduced here in 1542 (at the end of his life therefore) and
that the sitter was then twenty-eight years old. His identity is not known
but the falcon presumably indicates that he was a nobleman.

The Netherlands have never owned many of Holbein's works. Four of
them of high quality, however, were transferred by Prince William III
from England to The Hague after he had become King of England. After
his death they remained part of the Orange Collections until King William I
of the Netherlands in 1816 donated them to the Mauritshuis.

ANTONIO MORO (ANTHONIS MOR VAN DASHORST)
(1519–1575)

PORTRAIT OF SIR THOMAS GRESHAM   Panel
Rijksmuseum No. 1673 B 1   Height 90 cm. (35³/₈″)
                                   Width 75.5 cm. (29³/₄″)

In Moro's work the Renaissance Art of the Northern Netherlands reaches its international level. Anthonis Mor van Dashorst, born and bred at Utrecht, disciple of Jan van Scorel, went out into the world and began to make a reputation in Antwerp. Before long he was the favourite portrait painter of the Court and the aristocracy. He travelled to Italy and Portugal and was sent to England to paint the bride of the young Prince Philip, Queen Mary Tudor. Later he followed his prince to Spain. Utrecht, where his family remained, was forgotten; under the foreign-sounding name of Antonio Moro the artist acquired fame abroad. In the meantime his thorough Utrecht apprenticeship was by no means forgotten, but the artist's outlook widened as a result of all these journeys, which none of his fellow-countrymen artists before him had made. He acquired a grace and self-assurance which made his work restful; but above all he was a man with a sense for what is called distinction. The subjects of his portraits look quietly at the viewer, but as though from a distance. That distance they always keep – the distance the perfect courtier (like Holbein) always observes. It is not his place to embark on a psychological analysis of the faces posing before him. He never becomes intimate with them. But his portraits are certainly always good likenesses. Did he perhaps make them a little more beautiful, nobler, more dignified than they were in reality, and was that one of the secrets of his success?

Moro must have painted Sir Thomas Gresham's portrait shortly before 1566. Gresham lived from 1519 to 1579. He was a prominent and prosperous English merchant, founder of the London Stock Exchange and of Gresham College. He was also the representative of the trade interests of the English Crown in the South Netherlands. It is there that Moro must have painted him. The identification of the figure is based on its likeness to a portrait of Gresham in the National Portrait Gallery in London.

In the eighteenth century the painting belonged to Sir Robert Walpole's collection at Strawberry Hill. In 1779 it was acquired by Katharine II for the Hermitage at St Petersburg. In 1931 it was bought by the Rijksmuseum aided by the Rembrandt Society.

116

DIRCK JACOBSZ (1495–1567)
PORTRAIT OF POMPEJUS OCCO   Panel
Rijksmuseum No. 1290 A 1   Height 66 cm. (26″)
                                                  Width 54 cm. (21¹/₄″)

The head of a not very pleasant person looks penetratingly at us, while the fingers of his plump right hand elegantly hold a red and white carnation and the finger tips of the left hand rest almost caressingly on a human skull. That is how Dirck Jacobsz portrayed Pompejus Occo for us; a successful merchant who, judging from his face, must have been hard-headed in business, cunning, without many scruples but who in his leisure acted as a Maecenas and knew how to enjoy the refined spirit of the humanists: Amsterdam's first *mercator sapiens*. He already belongs to the upper class; of this his clothing is witness, especially the tabard trimmed with exquisite fur and, last but not least, the family coat of arms which hangs on a tree trunk, almost like a gay fruit, in the right-hand top corner of the panel. The town in the background is not situated on either the Amstel or the IJsel. It is a view based on the imagination of the painter, and placed in a mountainscape equally the product of fantasy.

In its conception the painting shows certain resemblances to the great German art of portraiture of the same generation. This is hardly surprising in the portrait of a man who was in regular touch with the Fuggers. But on the other hand, the flowing method of painting, nowhere inclining towards a linear style, is genuinely Dutch, and so are the restful composition and reserved colouring. Pompejus Occo originated from East Friesland. He was born about 1483 and died in 1537. In his time he was the most important wholesaler and banker in Amsterdam. He furthermore possessed a fine library and corresponded with prominent humanists. From a letter by the scholar Alardus of Amsterdam we learn that Occo was exceedingly proud of his humanism, which the portrait appears to confirm.

How the painting left the hands of the Occo family we do not know. Presumably it used to hang in the board room of the almshouse of the Occo family in Amsterdam. In 1895, at the sale of Doetsch in London, it went to the collection of Richard Kaufmann of Berlin, which was sold in 1917 when Mrs C. von Pannwitz of Bennebroek, Holland, acquired the panel. From her estate it was in 1957 bought for the Rijksmuseum from the Jonkheer John Loudon legacy.

118

PIETER BRUEGHEL THE ELDER
(1525/1530–1569)

THE TOWER OF BABEL   Panel
Boymans-van Beuningen Museum
Height 60 cm. (25⅝")
Width 74.5 cm. (29⅜")

The building of the Tower of Babel was not a
frequent subject until the Renaissance. However,
shortly before Brueghel painted this picture, the
Amsterdam artist Cornelis Anthonisz had made
an engraving of the tower's destruction. The
architecture of Brueghel's tower is so similar to
this engraving that the derivation of his version
from it does not seem at all unlikely. Both artists
depicted a massive tower something like the
Babylonian Temple. In the sixteenth century they
had presumably not themselves seen this building
or its ruins. They only knew these monuments by
tradition, which enabled them to substitute for
the true rectangular shape a circular one with a
spiral ascent round the tower. Heavy Near Eastern
minarets probably served them as further examples. The whole construction was supported
by an extensive system of Roman arches.

Brueghel made his tower colossal by placing it
in an extensive landscape, painted like a miniature.
There is a river on the right – perhaps the
Scheldt near Antwerp – with a quay at which
ships are docked bringing material for the
great work. More than seven thousand figures
have been counted engaged in the task. The
building has already reached the clouds (a detail of
treatment also found in the Anthonisz engraving).
The extreme refinement, in no way hindering the
grandiose vision, makes this painting one of the
glories of Brueghel's work. From Carel van Man-
der's *Book of Painters* we know that the painting was in the collections of
Emperor Rudolf II at Prague in about 1600. As appears from a coat of
arms painted on the back, it belonged in the eighteenth century to Elisabeth

Farnese of Parma, wife of King Philip V of Spain. In the twentieth century it was sold by a dealer to Mr D. G. van Beuningen; with his collection it was bought in 1958 by the Boymans-van Beuningen Museum.

JOOS DE MOMPER (1564–1635)
LANDSCAPE WITH WILD BOAR HUNT   Panel
Rijksmuseum No. 1641 A 5   Height 121 cm. (47⁵/₈")
                                                 Width 196.5 cm. (77¹/₄")

This wild boar hunt by Joos de Momper shows the extent to which he drew on fantasy. The brown rocks which arise almost unattainably high to left and right are steeper than any which can actually be found in the Southern Netherlands or even in the Alps. One has to go to the foot of the Greek Pindus to find such inaccessible rock-formations but neither De Momper nor any of his fellow-painters had ever been there. In between, immensely broad, stretches the river landscape wherein many ships move. They are mainly sailing ships but in front lie three galleys in the harbour. The little town is reminiscent of a Netherlands fortification at the Meuse, for instance that of Hoei, although the ground is hillier. From the bastion on the middle plane, on which stand bronze cannons (one of them fires a salute to the ships), blows the old Burgundian flag with the red Cross of St Andrew on a white field. It was under this flag that the Spaniards generally waged the Eighty-Years War in the Netherlands. There are also German elements in the scene, in particular the tall pine tree growing on the extreme left. But the two green lanes may well be of Dutch origin. They are a prelude to the landscape art of Rubens, as it were. Typically South-Netherlandish is the Renaissance château on the high mountain top in the right-hand upper corner of the panel. It is built of red brick but the gate, the balustrade and the arcades are of white grooved stone as are the frames and the decorations of the latticed windows. The hunting-party, too, is Dutch. Again a motif occurs which was also popular with Rubens and his school. Perhaps these figures are by the hand of Sebastian Vrancx (1573–1647). Compared with the vastness of nature they are correct but small. They are upholsterings, fitted into the great whole, as are the mills, churchess, trees, citadels, flocks and so many more details which together give it its vivacity, its colour accents, spots of light and shade, making the work an enthralling peep-show.

The panel belongs to De Momper's early work. It is one of the Rijksmuseum's most recent acquisitions, bought in 1958 from a Belgian art dealer.

PIETER AERTSZ, called *LANGE PIER* (1509–1575)
THE ADORATION OF THE SHEPHERDS (fragment)   Panel
Rijksmuseum No. 6   Height 90 cm. (35⅜″)
                                                        Width 60 cm. (23⅝″)

When Pieter Aertsz, after fruitful years of apprenticeship in Antwerp,
returned in 1555 or 1556 to his native town of Amsterdam, he was soon
– and rightly – a celebrated master to whom the most important commissions
available were given. Thus he was invited to paint a large altar piece for
the New Church, of which *The Adoration of the Shepherds* is the centre
panel. It attracted much admiration and, above all, for that part in which
these is a wonderfully realistic ox-head.

Almost all of this main work of the artist was destroyed in 1566 at the
time of the Iconoclasm. Seen in the larger context of Dutch history the
iconoclastic outbreak may have been an inevitable necessity or an in-
escapable fate which had to be suffered to make way for new ideas; but to
those dedicated to the fine arts it remains a regrettable episode which
caused incalculable damage to Holland's national heritage of art and made
a gap in the history of art which posterity can only bridge with difficulty.

Only a small fragment from Pieter Aertsz' masterpiece – the one most
admired – has been spared. It is not known how it escaped destruction.
Being the property of the city it was taken to the Town Hall, where it
was hung in the Orphans' Room. When this building was burnt down on
7th July 1652, the fragment was once again saved. This beautiful fragment
is therefore not only important as a work of art but, on account of the
events related here, as an historic relic of old Amsterdam. In 1885 the
town lent it to the Rijksmuseum.

JACOPO ROBUSTI, called *IL TINTORETTO* (1518–1594)

THE ANNUNCIATION — Two canvases

Rijksmuseum No. 2302 E 4 — each Height 115 cm. (45¹/₄″)

Width 93 cm. (36⁵/₈″)

The many religious paintings of Jacopo Robusti for the most part are still to be found in the churches and convents for which they were painted. There are, however, two canvases of the *Annunciation* at the Rijksmuseum. They were ordered to decorate the organ of San Benedetto in Venice, together with two other pictures representing Jesus and the Woman of Samaria, now in the Uffizi at Florence.

The two works here reproduced remained in the church of San Benedetto

126

until 1739. Count Francesco Algarotti, the author and scholar, of Venetian birth but well known abroad, bought them in 1746. He helped to form the collection of Auguste III of Saxony, but he probably bought these paintings for himself. They were afterwards in the collection of Prince Torlonia. They passed through dealers' hands to the Van Beckenrath collection in Berlin, and then to that of Professor Otto Lanz in Amsterdam. After the second world war, the Dienst voor's Rijks Roerend Kunstbezit lent them to the Rijksmuseum.

CAREL VAN MANDER (1548–1606)
THE DANCE ROUND THE GOLDEN CALF
Frans Hals Museum No. 204 b

Canvas
Height   99.5 cm.   (39¼″)
Width 216.5 cm.   (85¼″)

For his *Dance round the Golden Calf* Van Mander took his inspiration
from the tryptych of the same subject by Lucas van Leyden (page 104)
which, as we know from his *Book of Painters,* he greatly admired. He
copied Lucas's composition in outline, the wide, fantastic landscape with
mountains and trees, the idea of concentrating most attention on the
feasting Israelites in the foreground whereas the adoration of the idol was
pushed back to the second plane and Moses' figure was lost even more in
the background. But as a Protestant Van Mander substituted a rectangular
panel for the triptych thus making it a secular painting rather than a
devotional one. Now the artist could, without becoming objectionable, revel
uninhibitedly in the portrayed of noisy enjoyment, gay colours and mannered elegance. The result therefore differed strongly from the example set
three-quarters of a century previously.

   The painting, which is dated 1602, was bought in 1952 from the London
art market by the Frans Hals Museum.

ABRAHAM BLOEMAERT (1564–1651)
THE PREACHING OF JOHN THE BAPTIST   Canvas
Rijksmuseum No. 525 A 2   Height 139 cm. (54³/₈″)
                                                 Width 188 cm. (74″)

Long observation of a mannerist painting is needed before the main theme
can be distinguished. Abraham Bloemaert composed this painting following
mannerist principles. We notice in turn the fertile green landscape, the
central group of figures, and those on the left; only finally do we see
St John himself standing in the shade of a copse. This is an altogether
curious interpretation of the desert of Judaea where, according to the Bible
(Matthew 3:1) the Baptist preached.

The painting must have been done about 1600. In 1671 it belonged to
Henrik Houmes at Medemblik, then to Anthony de Rok at Hoorn. The
Rijksmuseum bought it in 1950 in London.

AMBROSIUS BOSSCHAERT (ca. 1565–1621)
Flowers   Panel
Mauritshuis No. 679   Height 64 cm. (25¹/₄″)
                                              Width 46 cm. (18¹/₈″)

Ambrosius Bosschaert was one of the Protestant painters of the Southern
Netherlands who in 1585 fled to Zeeland, where there was religious free-
dom. He thus brought to the north the Flemish style of flower painting. In
general he did not paint from nature but composed imaginary bouquets,
sometimes of flowers which are never in season together. We usually pass by
these inaccuracies, for Bosschaert's brush gives his arrangements a pleasing
distinction; he became famous in the United Netherlands. This picture was
bequeathed to the Mauritshuis by A. A. des Tombe in 1903.

SALOMON MESDACH
(active at the beginning of the seventeenth century)
PORTRAIT OF ANNA BOUDAEN COURTEN   Panel
Rijksmuseum No. 1541   Height 96 cm. (37³/₄")
                                              Width 70 cm. (27⁵/₈")

Salomon Mesdach was the artistic chronicler of Zeeland's golden age in the first half of the seventeenth century. We know little about him except from his paintings. Apparently simple, they are also subtle and masterly, showing his harmonious spirit and psychological insight. In 1620 he painted *Anna Boudaen Courten* (1599–1621), and her husband *Jacob Pergens*. These portraits remained in the family until in 1875 they were bequeathed to the Rijksmuseum by Jonkheer Jacob de Witte.

HENDRICK AVERCAMP called THE MUTE OF CAMPEN
(1585–1634)   Panel
WINTER SCENE
Rijksmuseum No. 392   Height   77.5 cm. (30¹/₂")
                                           Width 132   cm. (52")

The gay, abandoned swing of skaters over the ice was a joy to Hendrick
Avercamp. His mind was captivated by everything connected with Dutch
fun on ice. Merrily the couples glide hand-in-hand over the polished track.
Men strike out well with their legs. Others skate four abreast. A boy has
fallen on his stomach. There are peasant women, in their typical clothes,
and elegant ladies; there are toddlers and vain dandies, their hats with
enormous plumes tilted on their heads. One sees horse-drawn sleighs and
sledges passing by. A few figures are playing 'kolf', the old game which
was certainly known in the Netherlands by the beginning of the fifteenth
century, went from there to Scotland and then, by way of England, became
popular all over the world, to return finally to the Netherlands under the
anglicized, meaningless name of 'golf'. The sky is overcast. It looks as
though clouds are beginning to gather. Presently a mass of snow will
probably fall.

To the side lie the church and brick houses of a village, quiet under the
snow. Hungry crows sit on the roofs and in the trees. The front of the
brewery on the waterside has been embellished with the coat of arms of
Antwerp. This is certainly no coincidence for it all looks very Flemish here.
The whole idea stems directly from Brueghel's tradition. But in Avercamp's
work everything is finer, more stylish and precise; the colours and shapes
are less exuberant, more reserved; life is calmer than was usually the case
with the 'Peasant' Master. The temperament of the Dutchman differs from
that of the Fleming in treating the same subject. In his winter landscape,
carried out in detail like a miniature, Avercamp really stood nearer the
representations of January, as depicted in late-medieval breviaries where
the winter theme had its origin, than to Pieter Brueghel.

The painting originates from the collection of G. de Clerq of Amsterdam
and was in 1897 bought by the Rijksmuseum with the help of the Rembrandt Society.

PETER PAUL RUBENS (1577–1640)
ACHILLES SLAYING HECTOR   Panel
Boymans-van Beuningen Museum No. 389 e   Height 44   cm. (17³/₈″)
Width 51.5 cm. (20¹/₄″)

About 1626–1627 – the exact date is not known – Rubens painted a series
of eight sketches representing scenes from the life of Achilles, of which seven
are now the property of the Rotterdam Museum, whilst the eighth is in the
Whitcomb Collection at Detroit. They were meant as designs for tapestries.
As the weaving technique entailed showing the scenes on the tapestries in
reverse, the figures on the sketches are all left-handed. The person who
commissioned the work was probably the wealthy Antwerp silk- and carpet-
dealer Daniel Fourment, Rubens' future father-in-law. The theme was derived
from the stories of Homer, Virgil, Pausanias and Statius. The first scene
shows Thetis submerging her new-born son in the Styx. Then follow the
boy's education by the Centaur Chiron, the tale of Achilles with the
daughters of Lycomedes; his deeds during the Trojan War; his wrath
against Agamemnon; Thetis' request to Vulcan to forge some armour for her
son; the struggle between Achilles and Hector; and the death of the hero
himself.

The sketch reproduced opposite represents the penultimate event. Hector
has fallen and is pierced with a lance by Achilles. The figure gliding in the
air is Athene, the goddess-protector of Achilles; the gate in the background
indicates Troy.

In contrast with many of his large paintings, Rubens painted these rapid
sketches entirely by his own hand. They are exquisite examples of the
untrammelled force of imagination, the suppleness and fluency of his brushwork and the certainty of aim by which the Antwerp master roused his
figures to life and gave them character.

The eight sketches were mentioned in 1643 in the inventory of Daniel
Fourment at Antwerp. They subsequently appeared in the inventory of the
estate of Jan Baptista Anthoine (died 1687) at Antwerp. In 1724 they were
owned by Dr Richard Mead (London sale of 20th–21st March 1754), the
buyer being Mr Johnson. They then appeared in the sale of Fulk Greville
(18th November 1794, no. 49). Six of them then became the property of
A. H. Smith-Barry (later Lord Barrymore), of Marbury Hall, Northwick,
Cheshire. The Barrymore sale held in London on 21st June 1933, no. 28–33.
Donation from D. G. van Beuningen to the Boymans Museum in 1933.

PETER PAUL RUBENS (1577–1640)

EVENING LANDSCAPE   Panel

Boymans-van Beuningen Museum

Height 49.5 cm. (19¹/₂″)

Width 54.7 cm. (21¹/₂″)

Besides his many commissions for portraits, altar-pieces and other religious and mythological subjects, Rubens also painted landscapes. He enjoyed country life and willingly played his part as squire at his Château of Het Steen, near Mâlines. And how could Rubens, with his great gifts and wide interests escape being influenced by Pieter Brueghel's landscape art? Rubens painted more than forty large landscapes, which are among his most important works.

Interest in his landscapes grew rapidly. Prints by Schelte à Bolswert and others after Rubens' principal landscape made them even better known.

To people his landscapes, Rubens drew exquisite sketches of peasants at work, of cattle, groups of trees, and incidental subjects such as carts, gates and fences. But his vision went beyond this thorough grasp of details to create the atmosphere of each scene, whether sunny or, as this landscape is, in shadow but for the golden rays of a sunset which touch the trees and hills.

A small *Evening Landscape* by Rubens is mentioned in the collection of George Villiers, second Duke of Buckingham. This may be the painting here reproduced, about which it is certain that it was later (1841) in the collection of the Marquis of Camden. It appeared at the sale of Samuel Rogers (3rd May 1855), after which it passed to the collections of Thomas Baring, the Earl of Northbrook, and F. Koenig at Haarlem. After the second world war it was acquired by the Rijksdienst voor Roerend Kunstbezit which lent it to the Boymans-van Beuningen Museum.

PETER PAUL RUBENS (1577–1640)
THE PROCESSION TO CALVARY   Panel
Rijksmuseum No. 2065   Height 74 cm. (29$^{1}/_{8}$")
                              Width 55 cm. (21$^{5}/_{8}$")

Rubens' large altarpieces were for two centuries the Roman Catholic ideal of ecclesiastical art, often imitated in Belgium and abroad. Until the end of his life Rubens painted these colossal canvases, including this one for the abbey church of Affligham, commissioned in 1639 and placed in position on 8th April 1637. It shows the Procession to Calvary, and since 1815 has been in the Musée Royale, Brussels. Several sketches preceded its final execution, in each of which the positions and attitudes of the figures are different. The sketch in the Rijksmuseum is probably the one submitted by the artist to those who commissioned it in 1634. Another sketch in grisaille was engraved by Paulus Pontius in 1632 (now the property of Mrs M. Q. Morris, London), while a third, now hanging in the Copenhagen Museum, must be of a later date. Rubens had worked on this subject from about 1615, as could be seen from a sketch formerly in the Warsaw Museum.

The representation of *The Procession to Calvary* conforms to tradition – it could hardly be otherwise, with such a theme – but its execution, its movement and the feeling for the whole composition and each separate figure, are Rubens' own creation. The figure of the fallen Christ is characteristic of Rubens. On the right are strong men who hold up the heavy cross, one of them, no doubt, Simon of Cyrene (Luke 22:26). The kneeling figure on the left is Veronica, portrayed as a blonde Flemish peasant woman, who wipes Christ's face with her kerchief (a legend which is not in the Bible and only dates from the eleventh century). Behind her we recognise Mary and John. Surrounding the central figure of the prostrate Christ on the path to Golgotha is a turbulent crowd of Roman soldiers, women and children. A heavy sky of menacing clouds harmonises dramatically with the violent movement of the whole scene. On the right the sketch has been somewhat reduced.

The painting was successively in the sales of J. Meyers (Rotterdam 1722), J. de Roore (The Hague, 1747), Therese van Halen (Antwerp 1749) and Van de Marck (Amsterdam 1773). In 1781 Sir Joshua Reynolds admired it at the house of the collector Van Heteren at the Hague. Together with his collection it was in 1809 acquired by the Rijksmuseum.

ANTHONY VAN DYCK (1599–1641)

PORTRAIT OF QUINTIJN SIMONS

Mauritshuis No. 242

Canvas

Height 98 cm. (38⁵/₈″)

Width 84 cm. (33¹/₈″)

Quintijn Simons, a native of Brussels, was a painter by profession. History-painting was his speciality but this brought him no undying glory; as an artist Simons has long ago been forgotten. His name is now only known thanks to the fine portrait made of him by Van Dyck. Through this he belongs to the group of figures who have meant little or nothing in history but derive their fame only from the greatness of the artist who painted them. Who would ever have heard of Frans Banningh Cock if he had not been painted by Rembrandt as the central figure of *The Nightwatch*? Who thinks of Doña Isabel Cobos de Porcel without bringing Goya's portrait of her to mind? Who knows Madame Rivière but through Ingres' brush, and who knows the short-lived Spanish infant Don Balthasar Carlos but from Velasquez' vision?

The portrait of Quintijn Simons was probably painted in 1634 or 1635 when van Dyck resided at Brussels. It became a simple, not too colourful picture. The person represented stands cloaked in a sober but distinguished black coat before a brown wall. But how well has the figure been character-ised! The excessively heavy moustache has been elegantly stroked upwards, the goatee beard has been cut punctiliously, the fairly long hair which is hanging down has been carefully combed, everything to lend his exterior a semblance of importance which is completely and hopelessly lacking from the face itself. For Simons appears to us here as an insignificant man, a well-groomed but thoroughly unimportant figure. He appears nervous. He gazes uncertainly around without apparently looking for anything in particular. The fingers of the right hand in a mannered posture grip the coat tensely. With great virtuosity Van Dyck has arranged the many narrow folds of the big, soft collar and white cuffs to take part in this animated composition.

This canvas must already have been appreciated for its artistic merit at an early date. In the eighteenth century at any rate, it was no longer a family possession but belonged to the collection of the Dutchman Govert van Slingelandt. Later it was in the cabinet of Prince William V and after that, with his collections, it entered the Mauritshuis.

ADRIAEN BROUWER (1605 or 1606–1638)
PORTRAIT OF JAN DE DOOD   Panel
Boymans-van Beuningen Museum   Height 19.5 cm. (7³/₄″)
                                      Width 12   cm. (4³/₄″)

When Adriaen Brouwer was born at Oudenaarde in 1605 or 1606, Brueghel, 'The Peasant', had been dead for almost half a century, but his cherful, gay scenes of country-life still attracted great interest everywhere. How Brouwer came into contact with Brueghel's art we do not know but it is certain that it inspired him to become in his turn a painter of peasants, raw and true to life. In the same period a different style of portraying country-life was also known: that of elegant, lightly-dressed shepherds and shepherdesses with flowered crooks and big hats, playing the flute and courting in the shade of decorative copses with their woolly, cleanly-washed little sheep nearby. Brower did not like these charming but unrealistic intellectual stage and drawing-room portrayals, derived from reading poems like Virgil's *Bucolica* or its contemporary imitations. He was attracted by reality. His peasants are far from elegant. They are short and stocky, they wear simple clothes, the men are unshaven, the women heavy and fat; they drink and smoke (Equal sins! Did not the poet Adriaen Poirters call smoking 'drunkenness'?); they shriek, they fight; they embrace one another spontaneously and gruffly with both arms. Brouwer's peasants are people living close to the earth in poorish, loam huts. He observed them directly from the life. They seem to come from the same Brabant country as those of Brueghel, even when Brouwer moved to Amsterdam and later, in or shortly before 1628, to Haarlem. There he worked in Frans Hals' studio. They had in common a direct vision of humanity and a bold brushstroke. Later Brouwer returned to the South Netherlands where Teniers the Younger became his successor. He died, at thirty years of age, in Brueghel's town, Antwerp.

The painting by Brouwer in the Boymans-van Beuningen Museum can best be described by the French expression *pris sur le vif;* in every stroke of the brush, in every touch, life sparkles. The panel is known as the portrait of Jan de Dood. The Rotterdam Museum acquired it in 1958 with the D. G. van Beuningen Collection.

BARTOLOME ESTEBAN MURILLO (1618–1682)

Madonna with Child   Canvas

Rijksmuseum No. 1688 A 1   Height 190 cm. (74³/₄″)

Width 137 cm. (53⁷/₈″)

This impressive painting was bought by William I for the Mauritshuis some time before 1826, a choice typical of current taste. The State already owned a small work by Murillo, an Annunciation. Thereafter he was out of favour; later generations, less prone to emotionalism than the Romanticists, were often not able to appreciate Murillo's art at its full value. In any event, most Protestant Netherlanders probably found him too 'Catholic'; their regrettable ignorance of Spanish art played them false. Since 1948 the *Madonna with Child* has been lent by the Mauritshuis to the Rijksmuseum.

144

PHILIPPE DE CHAMPAIGNE (1602–1674)

Portrait of Jacobus Govaerts

Rijksmuseum No. 688 D 1

Canvas

Height 135 cm. (53¹/₈″)
Width 108 cm. (42¹/₂″)

Champaigne was born in Brussels where he received his training as a painter, but in 1621 he left for Paris to complete his studies there. Only seven years later he was appointed court painter. In 1665 he painted a former compatriot, Jacobus Govaerts, then twenty-nine, wearing a white lace-trimmed surplice, a bonnet in one hand, in the other a staff crowned with a silver Madonna statuette, the token of his dignity as Master of Ceremonies. The painting was bought in 1823 by King William I from General Rottiers for the Mauritshuis. In 1927 it was lent to the Rijksmuseum.

145

GERARD HONTHORST (1590–1656)
PORTRAIT OF PRINCE FREDERICK HENDRIK
AND AMALIA OF SOLMS-BRAUNFELS   Canvas
Mauritshuis No. 104   Height 213   cm. (83⁷/₈″)
                                             Width 201.5 cm. (83¹/₄″)

Of the seventeenth-century rulers of the House of Orange Frederick
Hendrik was the greatest Maecenas. Even in his youth when he lived with
his mother in the palace in the Noordeinde, The Hague, he ordered paintings to decorate the walls of his rooms. Later, after 1625 when he was
married and had become 'Stadtholder' he had a whole series of palaces built
and decorated with the help of his wife Princess Amalia. In this atmosphere
the great portrait of the Prince and Princess of Orange was painted, in 1637
or shortly afterwards. On the left stands the Stadtholder in the prime of
life – he was born in 1584 – in full armour, with the baton of commander-
in-chief in his hand and wearing the English Order of the Garter. We see
him as a forceful man, aware of his position and power and his wife as an
intelligent and no less self-assured weman. Her black dress is adorned with
a collar and cuffs of exquisitely woven lace and she wears a fortune in
pearls on her breast and in her hair. The red curtain with a gold-flowered
background, which recurrs in Honthorst's portraits, is held up by a tasselled
rope allowing us to see a flat Dutch landscape where an army camp is
pitched. Strangely this is behind the Princess not her husband. Gerard
Honthorst was already famous when he painted this large canvas. For his
candlelight effects he had been given in Italy the nickname of Gherardo
della Note, but soon after his return to the Netherlands he abandoned the
method to concentrate an portrait-painting. A short stay in England in
1628 may have contributed to this decision. In 1637 he was enrolled as
member of the St Luke's Guild at The Hague, about the same time therefore
as he painted this great double portrait. It was intended for Constantyn
Huygens, the faithful secretary of the Prince of Orange and was placed
over the mantel in a ground-floor room of the handsome living-quarters the
latter had built for himself at The Hague near where the Ministry of
Justice now stands. In 1800 however, the portrait was already in the
National Art Gallery. For a considerable time it had – wrongly – been hung
under the name of Michiel van Mierevelt.

FRANS HALS (between 1581 and 1585–1666)
THE REPAST OF THE OFFICERS OF THE ST JORISDOELEN   Canvas
Frans Hals Museum No. 124   Height 179 cm. (70½″)
Width 257.5 cm. (101¼″)

In the same year as the officers of the St Adriaansdoelen, those of the
Jorisdoelen had themselves painted at table by Hals. Here also the Colonel,
Burgomaster Aernout Druyvesteyn sits on the far left no doubt by a window
when the canvas was hung so that his figure would be in the best light.
Again the three captains are seated naturally round the table: next to the
Colonel sits Nicolaes Verbeek, then Michiel de Wael with an empty glass
in his hand and on the right Nicolaes Le Febure. Two of the lieutenants,
Jacob Pietersz Olycan and Frederik Koning, sit behind the table. The third,
Cornelis Boudewijnsz, has got up and approaches the Colonel on the
extreme left. The three other figures are the standard-bearers and the
landlord (standing in the background, second from right).

The painting was made for the large hall of the St Jorisdoelen.

FRANS HALS (between 1581 and 1585–1666)
REPAST OF THE OFFICERS OF THE ST ADRIAANSDOELEN   Canvas
Frans Hals Museum No. 125   Height 183 cm. (72″)
                                             Width 266.5 cm. (105″)

When in 1627 the officers of the St Adriaansdoelen in Haarlem commissioned Frans Hals to paint their portraits, he treated the traditional
theme in a highly personal way. The gentlemen are a lively group sitting
rather nonchalantly round the table. On the left, under the window and
in the best light, is the Colonel, the Haarlem Burgomaster Willem Voogt.
In the centre are the three captains, Johan Schatter, Gilles de Witt
(wearing a hat) and Willem Warmond. The three lieutenants, Outgert
Akersloot, Mattheys Haaswindius and Nicolaas van Napels (wearing a
hat) have been placed behind the table, on the extreme left. Those of lesser
rank, the fiscal Johan Damius and three standard-bearers, stand around
them. In the background the landlord of the Doelen goes round with the
wine jug. The picture was painted for the St Adriaansdoelen at Haarlem. It
went to the Town Hall, and then in 1913 to the Frans Hals Museum.

149

FRANS HALS (between 1581 and 1585–1666)
THE JOLLY TOPER   Canvas
Rijksmuseum No. 1091   Height 81   cm. (31⁷/₈″)
                                        Width 66.5 cm. (26¹/₄″)

The sitter of this vivid portrait is as yet unknown. He may eventually be
found among the drinking circle of the brewer Michiel de Wael; the
latter is seen in Hals' picture of the *St Jorisdoelen* (1627) of which he was
captain, ostentatiously turning his wineglass upside down. Hals liked to
celebrate the virtues of wine as well as of beer.

This painting must have been painted about 1627. It was bought for
the Rijksmuseum in 1816 at the sale of Baroness van Leyen of Warmond.

(Please note that the text on pages 150 and 151 should be transposed.)

FRANS HALS (between 1581 and 1585–1666)
Laughing Boy with Beer Jug   Canvas
Boymans-van Beuningen Museum   Height 69.5 cm. (27¹/₂″)
                                                Width 58 cm. (22⁷/₈″)

Hals several times painted figures holding beer jugs or tankards. This
Laughing Boy is one of these. His fur hat suggests that he was a seaman
or a fisherman. The simple earthenware tankard with a pewter lid was in
common use in Holland at that time. The boy shows cheerfully that his
mug is empty, while a laughing friend looks on.

The painting is from Hals' light period and must date from about
1627–30. It belongs to the Almshouse Van Aarde at Leerdam and has been
lent to the Rotterdam Museum.

FRANS HALS (between 1581 and 1585–1666)
PORTRAIT OF A MAN AND HIS WIFE   Canvas
Rijksmuseum No. 1084   Height 140 cm. (55^1/$_8$")
                           Width 166.5 cm. (65^1/$_2$")

This happy husband and wife are not known by name
any more than *The Jolly Toper*. They must have been
from Haarlem. It is unlikely to be a self-portrait of the
artist or of his brother Dirck, as has sometimes been
suggested. These rosy-cheeked, simple, straightforward
types, painted with just the right touch, are thoroughly
Dutch and so is the high, bright-blue sky with its decorative white clouds. But the brilliant atmosphere of
an early summer's day, the villa, the fountain and the
statue in the garden behind stem directly from Italy.
The building is reminiscent (on a smaller scale) of the
architecture of a Roman country-house like the Villa
Doria-Pamphili; the fountain appears to have been
touched by the spirit of a Bernini. And on the right in
the foreground lies a fragment of an old Roman building which might have been taken straight from the
ruins of the Forum. Frans Hals, who never visited Italy
himself, obviously desired to demonstrate by all these
details that he was well abreast of everything considered
worthy, beautiful and modern in his time.

   That one should look for more than a simple attempt
to bring life to the scene is made clear by two additiond
items: the plants growing in front of the two sitters.
By the woman's feet an ivy tendril climbs upwards
while beside her husband grows a thistle. The painter,
living in a period which was passionately interested in
emblems and symbolism, undoubtedly meant to make
an allusion to the different characters of husband and
wife.

   The painting is one of the early works of Hals; it
must have been painted about 1621. The trees may have been
one of his collaborators at Haarlem, for example Pieter Molijn.

   The canvas came from the sales of Jan Six (Amsterdam 1702)
of Hillegom (Amsterdam 25th November 1851). In 1852 it b
property of the Rijksmuseum.

152

WILLEM PIETERSZOON BUYTENWECH (1591–1624)
Country Courtships
Rijksmuseum No. 668 B 1

Canvas
Height 56 cm. (22")
Width 70 cm. (27⅝")

Buytenwech's elegant painting of two couples in their best clothes does not give a representative picture of every-day life in the Netherlands at the beginning of the seventeenth century. It is more like a scene on the stage ridiculing the extravagant fashions which pleased the *jeunesse dorée* of that prosperous age. The coat of arms on the window embrasure is probably that of the Duvelandt van Rhoon family; the two ladies would then be the sisters of that name who married, at Haarlem in 1608, Dirc van der Nath and Johan de Bruyn van Buytenwech. This painting was given to the Rijksmuseum in 1926 by the Comissie tot Verkoop van Fotografieën.

JAN MIENSE MOLENAAR (1610–1668)

FAMILY GROUP

Frans Hals Museum No. 213 b

Panel

Height 61.5 cm. (24¹/₄″)
Width 80 cm. (31¹/₂″)

In contrast with Buytenwech's two eccentric couples, the members of Molenaar's unknown family group are simplicity itself. The composition contains elements of symbolism. The little boy blowing soap-bubbles was for contemporaries a clear-cut symbol of the shortness of life; the ticking clock similarly symbolises the flight of time. Even the music can be interpreted in the same way, for the sound of strings fades quickly ...

To judge from their clothes the couple whose portraits hang on the wall are of the preceding generation, who had already died by 1635 when Molenaar painted this family. The portraits are probably by Frans Hals, but they are lost. The Rijksdienst voor Roerend Kunstbezit lent this work to the Frans Hals Museum.

JAN DE BRAY (1627–1697)
TENDING THE ORPHANS
Frans Hals Museum No. 35

Canvas
Height 134.5 cm. (53")
Width 154 cm. (60⁵/₈")

The representation of the Seven Works of Charity had become a frequent subject by the end of the Middle Ages, especially in the Netherlands. The theme is taken from a *Life of Christ* by the monk Ludolphus of Saxony, inspired by a passage in St Matthew (25:35–46). By practising the Seven Works of Charity, namely: feeding the hungry, refreshing the thirsty, giving hospitality to strangers, clothing the naked, visiting the sick, taking care of prisoners, and, finally, burying the dead, the good Christian could aspire to heaven. After the Reformation Protestants no longer accepted Ludolphus' text. But the Dutch continued to exercise charity, doing through the Reformed what had formerly been done by the Roman Catholic Church. In this way Dutch towns got more orphanages, almshouses and charitable institutions than could be found in any other country in the world. There soon appeared in the decorations of these rooms of these institutions a new iconography, based on tradition but adapted to the changed circumstances. When Jan de Bray was commissioned in 1663 to execute a picture for the Orphanage of the Poor at Haarlem, the subject he chose was not new. Frans Pietersz de Grebber, amongst others, had used it in a picture (1620), now in the Frans Hals Museum. Nevertheless, de Bray's treatment of the theme is decidedly modern. He successfully created a synthesis of the old an new in a characterstically gay and balanced work.

On the left a woman dresses two poor children. She is helping a small boy to put on a new black jacket, with one red sleeve. This was the dress of the Haarlem orphans which they wore until the twentieth century. Another woman on the right is distributing bread, large slices such as the Dutch still eat today. An orphan girl – she can be recognised by her black dress with a red sleeve – has gratefully taken a thick slice of bread and butter. In the foreground a boy is eating happily while another is obviously pleased at putting on an orphan's dress. Behind the woman with the bread a pale boy is drinking from a pitcher. He is the only one to look pale – all the others are rosy-cheeked and round-faced. The composition of the painting is vivid and natural. By placing figures in front of the dais where charity is practised, de Bray gives the scene a depth completely in keeping with the Baroque ideas of his time. This painting has been in the Frans Hals Museum since 1913.

JOHANNES BOTH (1618 or later –1652)
ITALIAN LANDSCAPE WITH SKETCHERS   Canvas
Rijksmuseum No. 591   Height 187 cm. (73⅝″)
           Width 240 cm. (94½″)

More than the Italians themselves it was the foreign artists who, captivated by the natural beauty of the Apennines and the Roman campagna, painted them and made of them an ideal landscape. It is difficult to establish who contributed more to this, the French led by Claude Lorrain and Poussin, or the numerous Dutch 'Italianisers'. Jan Both was one of the first of these. In his large landscape in the Rijksmuseum the artist shows himself from behind in conversation with an Italian shepherd. He is no doubt making a sketch like his companion opposite him. A little further to the right, a group of travellers passes by: two mules are loaded with a litter, while three others follow with luggage, gazed at by some shepherds whose goats, on the left under the trees, are lying chewing the cud. But these figures are really incidental, doing no more than filling in the grandiose landscape. The setting sun envelops in a golden glow mountains, castles, and the mirror-like lake (probably Lake Trasimeno). The contours of the high rocks in the middle distance have become sharp but the bluish mountains on the horizon are already beginning to fade. The foreground is by now in shade, but under the high trees on the left falls a last sunray, giving for a moment remarkable fleeting depth to a few plants, humans and animals.

This concept of Italian nature was to remain an ideal, the true idyll in many countries of Europe for a very long time to come. Thus it is difficult to over-estimate the incentive given to the development of this type of landscape art by Jan Both and his followers.

This great picture is first mentioned at the sale of Quirijn van Biesum at Amsterdam in 1719; next at the sales of Pickfatt in Rotterdam in 1736 and Thomas Hamlet in London in 1833. Later it was part of the A. van der Hoop Collection at Amsterdam, who bequeathed it in 1854 to the town of Amsterdam. Since 1885 it has been lent by the town to the Rijksmuseum.

JAN VAN GOYEN (1595–1656)
VIEW ON THE MEUSE, DORDRECHT   Panel
Rijksmuseum No. 989   Height 55.5 cm. (21³/₄")
                                             Width 72 cm. (28³/₈")

Dordrecht was proud of being Holland's oldest town, the first to be granted
a charter. Did van Goyen know the glorious history of the town? Was the
monumental Great Church with its heavy uncompleted tower anything more
to him than part of a picture? Certainly a number of Dutch seventeenth-
century townscapes were inspired by local patriotism. This thoroughly
Dutch riverscape is dated 1648.

The painting came from the sales of J. van der Marck (1773); J. J. de
Bruyn (Amsterdam, 1798); A. van der Werff of Zindland (1811); A. Lacoste
(Dordrecht, 1832); the cabinet of J. Lambouts (Dordrecht, 1850); the collec-
tion of L. Dupper Wzn, who bequeathed it to the Rijksmuseum in 1870.

JAN VAN GOYEN (1596–1656)
Landscape with Two Oaks   Canvas
Rijksmuseum No. 990   Height 88.5 cm. (34³/₈″)
                                            Width 110.5 cm. (43¹/₂″)

Jan van Goyen was born in 1596 at Leyden. He lived and worked in this
town until some time between 1632 and 1634, when he moved to The
Hague. There he painted this picture in 1641. The canvas obviously takes us
to the edge of the dunes, possibly somewhere between The Hague and Leyden. To the left, in the middle distance, stretches the low ground along the
foot of the dunes. It is doubtful whether the place could be identified. Sometimes van Goyen painted his landscapes true to nature; at others not. The
painting was in the sale of A. Lacoste at Dordrecht in 1832; until 1850 in
the cabinet of J. Rombouts of Dordrecht; then in the collection of L. Dupper
Wzn of that town, who bequeathed it to the Rijksmuseum in 1870.

HENDRICK CORNELISZ VROOM (1566–1640)
THE SAILING OF EAST-INDIES MERCHANTMEN   Canvas
Rijksmuseum No. 2606 c   Height 103.5 cm. (40³/₄″)
                                               Width 198.5 cm. (78¹/₂″)

Hendrick Cornelisz Vroom opens the line of great Dutch marine painters.
Admittedly, he did not invent the genre but older pictures (on panel or as
prints) had been occasional pieces by masters who usually applied themselves to other subjects. Vroom, however, devoted most of his life to the
seascape.

Here he shows the sailing of a number of East-India ships on 1st May
1598. Three years previously Dutch ships had for the first time undertaken
the trip to the Far East. It was the beginning of an intensive and prosperous
trade. No wonder that this second voyage to the East drew great attention.
The Commodore's ship, *Mauritius,* sails majestically out of Marsdeep
followed by seven other ships. On the one side is the extreme tip of the
Dutch coast, on the other lie the dunes of the island of Texel. In the foreground, onlookers enliven the scene. A woman cries into a big white hand-
kerchief; in a rowing boat stands a trumpeter blowing a last farewell to
those leaving. Was it perhaps the 'Little Song of the Prince of Orange',
the Wilhelmus already familiar at that time, which was played on such
occasions? In 1930 the painting was donated to the Rijksmuseum by
Dr J. W. IJzerman of Wassenaar.

JAN VAN DE CAPPELLE (1626–1679)
THE STATE-BARGE GREETED BY THE HOME FLEET   Panel
Rijksmuseum No. 681   Height 64   cm. (25¹/₄″)
                                             Width 92.5 cm. (36¹/₂″)

The scene depicted on this painting would at first sight appear to be
realistic. Ships fired salutes and with broad gestures of the arms the crew
welcomed the occupants of the sloop rowing alongside, including the popular stadtholder, Prince Frederik Hendrik. But the artist himself can hardly
have seen this visit to the fleet, for the panel bears the date 1650 when
Frederik Hendrik had already been dead for three years. Thus Van de Capelle's scene is imaginary, possibly an *in memoriam* for the Prince, or just
an arresting scene without any historic or allegoric content, a very successful
portrayal of a mood. For this the painter consulted his master, Simon de
Vlieger, who in 1649 had painted a similar visit to the fleet by the Prince
(Akademie, Vienna); apparently a favourite theme, there was a second version by Van de Capelle (Boymans - van Beuningen Museum, Rotterdam).

   The painting is amongst the oldest possessions of the Rijksmuseum; in
1808 it was already in the National Museum at The Hague.

AERT VAN DER NEER (1603 or 1604–1677)

RIVERSCAPE IN WINTER

Rijksmuseum No. 1720

Canvas

Height 64 cm. (25¼")
Width 79 cm. (31⅛")

Van der Neer's ice scene shows similarities to as well as differences from that of Avercamp which is reproduced on page 133. They are alike, in the first place, in the theme as well as in its design, with the wide, frozen river full of skaters in the centre and the houses on the left, while the high sky is clouded. But Van der Neer was no maker of miniatures as was Avercamp. He was just as interested in the details of the figures but he painted them with a heavier brush. As a result his men became sturdier, more robust and less affected, but also less carefree. Their size increased somewhat, their numbers decreased considerably. Van der Neer added few women to his scene and no girls at all. Also missing are the peasant women in their flowery dresses. Thus there is considerably less variety although the 'kolf' game, sledge and horse-drawn sleigh remain. The simple village has now been replaced by a large town with numerous striking tall towers. Such a richly varied skyline did not exist anywhere in the Netherlands of those days. It is most like that of seventeenth-century Antwerp but the frozen river does not show any resemblance to the Scheldt.

With Van der Neer the world has become more respectable, broader in style, heavier in tone and form. Even the clouds and the sheafs of sunrays which halo the town share this quality. The dark tones of the tree trunks in the foreground accentuate it particularly. This new concept is an improvement over Avercamp, producing a wider vision. The branches in the foreground combine with the high trees on the right, the lower ones on the left, on the second plane, and finally the dark clouds in the sky, to provide a framework for the scene and weld it firmly into a whole.

This winterscape used to be in the collection of Edward Gray at Harringay; later, in 1839, with Brondgeest; and finally it became the property of A. van der Hoop of Amsterdam who in 1854 bequeathed it to the town. Since 1885 it has been loaned to the Rijksmuseum.

LOUIS LE NAIN (1593?–1648)
Two Girls   Canvas
Boymans-van Beuningen Museum No. 310   Height 41   cm. (16¹/₈")
                                              Width 30.3 cm. (12")

In the seventeenth century Dutch and Flemish realism was paralleled by
'bourgeois' painting in France; contacts certainly existed between the two.
The most important practitioners of this trend were the three brothers Le
Nain, Antoine (1588?–1646), Louis (1593?–1648) and Matthieu (1607?–1677).
They came from Laon where they must have received their first training
from a Dutch or Flemish artist. It is difficult to decide which paintings
belong to each brother. That shown here may be by the hand of Louis. In
1908 it was donated to the Rotterdam Museum by Adolphe Schloss.

166

BARTHOLOMEUS BREENBERG (1599/1600–between 1655 and 1659)
ITALIAN LANDSCAPE   Canvas
Mauritshuis No. 932   Height 51.3 cm. (20¹/₄")
                                            Width 78   cm. (30³/₄")

The present-day museum public, interested as it is in the old Dutch masters,
usually does not realise the extent to which in Dutch art of the seventeenth
century there was a conflict between native and international concepts.
Bartholomeus Breenberg was of the latter school. At Rome he came in contact with the German painter Adam Elsheimer, with Paul Bril, a native of
Antwerp, and worked with the Utrecht artist Cornelis Poelenburg. After his
return to Holland he was one of those who made sunny, southern landscapes
popular in Holland. He filled them out with picturesque fragments of real
buildings and ruins, imaginatively arranged. Here the wall of Aurelianus
which surrounded old Rome is placed beside fragments of architecture from
antiquity, but the mountains and the castle in the distance look as if they
have been remembered from a journey through the Alps. The painting was
in the collections of Lord Egerton, Thesiger and Alfred Brod in London
and was bought by the Mauritshuis in 1959.

JAN BAPTIST WEENIX (1621–before the end of 1663). The Visit by J
Rijks

The town in the distance, to the left of the centre, is Goa, an important
Portuguese settlement in India. The ships lying in front are Dutch and
blockade the town during one of the colonial wars which were forever
flaring up. The figure on the white horse is the Paymaster of the Fleet,
Johan van Twist who, as Ambassador of the United Netherlands East-
India Company, is going to pay a visit to the native king of neighbouring
Visiapur. The cloak of gold thread with which the ruler has honoured him

o Visiapur.   Canvas.   Height 101 cm. (36³/₄″).   Width 179 cm. (70¹/₂″).
A 1.

is already hanging over his shoulders. An Indian steward seated on a
beautiful black horse accompanies him. To the right, women and children
cheerfully greet the welcome guest. This event took place in 1637, but
Weenix's rendering owes much to the imagination, although the topography
of the town seems reliable. The artist himself had never been in the East.

   In 1953 the painting was bought by the Rijksmuseum.

PAULUS POTTER (1625–1654)
Horses in a Field
Rijksmuseum No. 1911

Panel
Height 23.5 cm. (9¹/₄″)
Width 30 cm. (11³/₄″)

This painting is not the most characteristic work by Potter. As a rule he limited himself to cabinet-pictures and his paintings of cattle were simple in design. Of a cheerful temperament, he liked to see the Dutch meadows with the sunlight pouring over them on a beautiful summer's day. Possibly his sunny vision was influenced by the art of the 'Italianisers' but during his short life he never visited the South. He usually placed the horizon very low, as it is only seen in the flat Dutch polders – an important step in the development of an individual Dutch vision of a landscape. *Horses in a Field* dates from 1649. The artist himself made an etching of it, with a few changes. Bought in 1833 by A. van der Hoop at the sale of Jonkheer J. Goll van Frankenstein at Amsterdam, in 1854 it was bequeathed to the city of Amsterdam and in 1885 lent to the Rijksmuseum.

KAREL DU JARDIN (1622–1678)

THE YOUNG SHEPHERD

Mauritshuis No. 760

Panel

Height 31.2 cm. (12¼″)

Width 37.6 cm. (14⅞″)

About the scene of this painting little can be said. Somewhere in Italy, probably in the Campagna, a shepherd boy plays with his dog. He has placed a basket with food and a barrel with drink by his side. A sheep and a goat are quietly chewing the cud and a lean white horse is grazing. Some bare bones (bottom, right) provide a foil. In the distance rises the bare massif, monumental and inaccessible, and above the deep-blue Italian sky. Between this background and the immediate foreground glides a minute bird of prey. Everything in this panel breathes peace. It is not dated. It must belong to the last period of the artist, who died in 1678 in Venice. Presented by J. Goudstikker of Amsterdam to the Mauritshuis, 1919.

JAN ASSELIJN (1610–1652)

THE THREATENED SWAN   Canvas

Rijksmuseum No. 382   Height 144 cm. (56³/₄″)

Width 171 cm. (67³/₈″)

In this painting a life-size swan, scolding loudly and violently clapping his wide-spread wings, defends his nest of eggs against the threat of a dog which comes swimming along from the left. It was the first work of art bought for Holland's oldest public museum, the National Art Gallery at The Hague. The Director, C. S. Roos, wrote on 11th June 1800 to Gogel, the representative of the Ministry of Finance, that he had bought it 'for next to nothing, namely for Fls. 95 – with premium and table-money Fls. 100.'

The subject, though not occurring often, can yet not be called rare. It was almost certainly not an original idea of Asselijn's. The vigorous composition and forceful painting suggest that this undated piece is among the late works of the artist. The clear, bluish colouring as well as the mountainscape which completes the horizon, are typical of the concepts of the 'Italianisers' among the North-Netherlandish painters, to which group Asselijn belonged. He had studied in Italy and had in Rome come under the influence of Claude Lorrain among others.

Later, the subject of the threatened swan was made into an allegory by inscribing under the bird the words *THE GRAND PENSIONARY,* on one of the eggs the word *HOLLAND* and above the dog the words *THE ENEMY OF THE STATE.* By 'The Grand Pensionary' was meant Johan de Witt who, when young, had written poems under the transparent nom de plume of 'Candidus'. The white swan was his family crest. The intention of the allegory is therefore plain even if the meaning of 'The Enemy of the State' remains unclear.

Jan Asselijn, however, can have possessed no knowledge of all this as he died before De Witt had been appointed Grand Pensionary and before the Republic became seriously threatened either from without or from within. It is not known who added the letters to the canvas but from the evidence it may be deduced that it came from the estate of Jean Deutz, a brother-in-law and great friend of De Witt, who, in honour of his great, much-admired brother-in-law, had Asselijn's painting, which he already possessed or possibly bought specially for the occasion, made into an allegory, in accordance with the spirit of the time. In 1800 after the Jean Deutz sale the canvas again came under auction in Amsterdam, in the Gildemeester Collection, and was bought for the National Art Gallery.

172

THOMAS DE KEYSER (1596 or 1597–1667)
PIETER SCHOUT   Copper
Rijksmuseum No. 1350   Height 86 cm. (33⁷/₈″)
                                               Width 69.5 cm. (27¹/₄″)

Impressive, life-size portraits of horsemen such as were popular with
most of the West European aristocracy in the seventeenth century, were
only rarely ordered in the 'bourgois' republic of the United Netherlands.
We know of only two: Rembrandt's vivid portrait of the Amsterdam
burgomaster's son Jacob de Graeff, riding at the head of a platoon of
horsemen before the coach of the young Prince William III (National
Gallery, London) and Potter's less ponderous, more dashing portrait of a
rider in the Six Collection at Amsterdam. Even in a smaller size more
suited to the dimensions of Dutch houses, few horsemen were painted. In
the seventeenth and eighteenth centuries the Dutch with the exceptions of
the well-to-do youth of Amsterdam, seem to have practised horsemanship
less than the noblemen of other countries. There were a few painters of
such subjects, Thomas de Keyser being the most important.

Pieter Schout, who had himself portrayed on horseback by De Keyser,
lived in Amsterdam from 1640 to 1669. The painting is dated 1660. In
the summer of that year the Prince of Orange who was not yet ten years
old, and who later became William III, paid an official visit to Amsterdam with his mother, Mary Stuart (daughter of Charles I). The city welcomed the princely company with great pomp. As happened often on
such occasions, a splendidly attired guard of horsemen, all important
townsmen, met the visitors and accompanied them on their festive entry.
One of the commanders of this cavalcade was the above mentioned Jacob
de Graeff; Pieter Schout was also among those taking part. Naturally
enough, he chose to pose in the handsome costume which he had been
wearing, and on the noble animal he had ridden, to commemorate an
event important in the eyes of his contemporaries. Thus originated one
of Thomas de Keysers's subtle little paintings, minute in detail, gay in
colouring, harmonious yet always lively in composition. The figure is
painted with great skill. Whether the landscape was added by the painter
himself, is not quite certain. Dr H. Schneider believes it is by Adriaen
van de Velde.

The portrait of Pieter Schout on horseback remained family property
until Jonkheer J. S. H. van de Poll bequeathed it on his death in 1880 to
the Rijksmuseum.

174

PIETER JANSZOON SAENREDAM (1597–1665)

St Mary's Church Utrecht   Canvas
Boymans-van Beuningen Museum No. 399   Height 110.5 cm. (43¹/₂″)
                                        Width 139   cm. (54³/₄″)

As the son of an engraver Pieter Saenredam had grown up in an artistic family circle and it was therefore not strange that he devoted his life to art. He became a painter and also architectural draughtsman to, among others, the architect Jacob van Campen, his fellow-townsman of Haarlem. Van Campen had also been trained as a painter but made his great reputation particularly by his buildings. Saenredam's pictures often make one wonder which art interested him most – painting or architecture. Besides these two, he had yet another interest: the Middle Ages. This deserves attention, for the first half of the seventeenth century cared little as a rule for what remained from the 'Gothic dirt', as Constantijn Huygens chose to express it once. Saenredam shared this remarkable mental disposition with van Campen; it does not even seem impossible that the latter induced him towards it. These three areas of interest are united in the painting of the Mariaplaats at Utrecht. The Church of Mary dated from Romanesque times. When the Reformation broke through, the building came to the Protestants but – strangely enough – the Chapter was allowed to continue as the worldly duties which the canons performed besides their spiritual tasks were not abolished. The only difference was that in future the gentlemen had to be members of the Dutch Reformed Church. This lent the church a halo of respectability throughout the entire seventeenth and eighteenth centuries, which may have been an additional reason for Saenredam choosing this time-honoured building as the subject of a painting.

It was a happy thought on the part of the artist not to place the church, which forms the main motif of the scene, in the centre of the canvas. Thus he avoided the stiffness to which the portrayal of such a flat façade seen from straight in front, might have led. Now the viewer's eye glides over the quiet, intimate little square on the left, then moves upward and reaches, by way of the two spires in the background, those of the 'Buurkerk' (Neighbour's Church) and the dome, the theme proper which, with the ascending lines of the roof of the transept, the chancel tower, the nave and finally the clock tower, closes off the composition. The heavy mass of the Romanesque structure also has a closed effect and it is indeed fitting in this arrangement that the door should be closed. After all, a Romanesque Church did not open its doors invitingly to the faithful. Rightly, therefore, the little figures which give life to the painting are

176

quite unconcerned with the church. They are interested in one another or immersed in their own thoughts. It is doubtful whether these discreet, but enlivening colour accents are the work of Saenredam himself. Their lively style seems to betray a different hand.

The canvas is dated 1663 but was painted after a drawing which Saenredam had already made in 1636 (Teylers Museum, Haarlem). The Church of Mary was pulled down in 1813.

The painting was bought by the Boymans Museum in 1872.

GERARD HOUCKGEEST (about 1600–1661)
INTERIOR OF THE NEW CHURCH AT DELFT
Mauritshuis No. 58

Canvas

Height 56 cm. (22″)
Width 38 cm. (15″)

Churches have always from olden times been painted by Dutch artists. In the later Middle Ages, they formed for Jan van Eyck, Rogier van der Weyden or Geertgen tot Sint Jans, a suitable background to Madonnas, the figures of saints or other religious scenes. In great measure they suggested the atmosphere of devotion which should emanate from such a piece. The Reformation secularised the church motif, as it did so many others, and elevated it from a stylish background for something that was considered more important to a subject worth portraying in itself. A whole group of Dutchmen now began to concentrate on it and Gerard Houckgeest was one of them. He was a native of The Hague but later moved to Delft. The two great medieval churches of that town were his most cherished theme. The painting in the Mauritshuis represents a view into the New Church which dates from the fourteenth and fifteenth centuries. Through the white-washed pillars is seen the tomb of Prince William I of Orange, the masterpiece of Hendrick de Keyser, which was erected in the years 1614–1622 by order of the States, in honour of the 'Father of the Fatherland', in the choir which had been lowered to floor level. It was the most beautiful tomb to adorn a Dutch church during Houckgeest's life. Both for this reason and because of the memory of the beloved prince which it honoured this monument enjoyed great popularity and the question arises whether Houckgeest, in his *Interior of the New Church*, intended to paint an undoubtedly picturesque church interior, or the tomb which had for every right-minded Dutchman so many historical associations. Above the monument hang gaily painted wooden coats of arms in honour of Prince William, his fourth wife Louise de Coligny and his sons Maurits and Frederik Hendrik. They all rest in the family vault which is under the tomb. These coats-of-arms unfortunately disappeared during the French Revolution. The tournament lances with standards on the walls were probably from princely funerals.

The viewer will also observe that naughty boys have drawn dolls in red chalk on the foot of one of the pillars!

The painting in the Mauritshuis is dated 1651. At the sale of J. van Kinschot of Delft on 21st July 1767 it was withdrawn. Shortly afterwards Prince William V bought the painting for his cabinet. With the rest of his collection it came to the Mauritshuis.

178

EMANUEL DE WITTE (about 1617–1692)

INTERIOR OF THE PORTUGUESE SYNAGOGUE IN AMSTERDAM   Canvas

Rijksmuseum No. 2698 A 3   Height 110 cm. (43¹/₄″)

Width   98 cm. (38⁵/₈″)

The Portuguese Synagogue is the most beautiful in Amsterdam and perhaps
in the whole of Europe. It was built by the Amsterdam surveyor and
master mason, Elias Bouman between 1671 and 1675. This was the period
when many Portuguese Jews, together with the Spanish ones, had achieved
great wealth there, after having been driven from the Iberian Peninsula
on account of their faith and having fled in large numbers to the Free
Republic of the Netherlands. Quite a few great gentlemen were among
them, noblemen sometimes, a few of whom could even boast blood relationship with the governing House of Braganza. They adapted themselves
well to their new fatherland and so it was possible for their house of
prayer to become a characteristic expression of the cool, reserved, stately
Dutch classicism which had little need of ostentation to express distinction.
The building was in the shape of a rectangular block. Four huge Ionic
pillars of sandstone support the three parallel wooden barrel-vaults. The
noble simplicity of the building, with the beautiful play of light through
the high windows did not fail to captivate Emanuel de Witte. The painting
became an exception among the work of the gifted painter of Calvinistic
whitewashed churches; as a rule he was not interested in modern buildings.

With loving brush he allows the sunlight to glide over the white pillars
and walls; he enlivens the monotony of the walls with the rhythmic
verticals of gay red curtaining and he plays, as it were, with the contrast
between the wide, sober white space and the crowd filling it. The tones
which predominate there are the brown of the dresses and the black of
the many big round hats which the men wear on their heads as prescribed
by the Jewish religion. But one figure shows up as being different from the
rest: a tall blond young man in a somewhat unusual light blue over-
coat with red trimmings and red stockings. He stands in the full light of
the foreground and his appearance is important as a foil to the effect of
depth in the painting. Brightly polished yellow copper candelabra with
decoratively bent arms give a further feeling of space. It is remarkable
that all this occurs on the lower half of the canvas; the top is almost
entirely taken up by the three enormous brown wooden barrel-vaults seen
in marked perspective and the heavily profiled architraves.

The painting came from the Kaiser Friedrich Museum at Berlin, was sold

to a Berlin art-dealer, became part of the Anton Jurgens Collection in London and was in 1949 bought on the London art market by the Rijksmuseum.

GERARD TER BORCH (1617–1661)
PORTRAIT OF GODARD VAN REEDE VAN NEDERHORST Copper
Rijksmuseum No. 573 A 6 Height 14.5 cm. (5³/₄")
Width 11 cm. (4³/₈")

PORTRAIT OF COUNT VAN PENARANDA Copper
Boymans-van Beuningen Museum Height 12 cm. (4³/₄")
Width 9 cm. (3¹/₂")

Gerard ter Borch deserves especial attention among miniature portrait
painters. His sitters were for the most part rulers or aristocrats, as here
Godard van Reede, Lord of Nederhorst (1588–1648) member of an old
Utrecht family. His pallor reflects his bad health; he died that year.

During his stay at Munster Ter Borch also painted the leader of the
Spanish delegation, Gaspar de Bracamonte y Guzman, Count of Penaranda
(1590–1676). What a difference between these two sitters, of about the
same age. Penaranda is in perfect health, graceful, elegant and alert. We
do not know when this portrait left his family's possession. In modern
times it was in the Kremer Collection, Paris, and the sale of E. Warneck,
Paris. It was bought in 1926 by D. G. van Beuningen at Rotterdam and
entered the Boymans-van Beuningen Collection in 1958.

GERARD TER BORCH
<small>LADY WRITING A LETTER</small>   Panel
Mauritshuis No. 797   Height 39   cm. (15³/₈″)
                                             Width 29.5 cm. (11¹/₂″)

Ter Borch is also well known for his fine interiors with figures, often
members of the artist's family. Thus the beautiful letter writer in the
Mauritshuis is probably his sister Gesina. The painting must have originated about 1655 or shortly afterwards. It comes from the auction of the
Duc de Choiseul (Paris, 6th April 1772), was later in the Six van Hillegom
Collection at Amsterdam, was bought at the Six auction (London, 16th October 1928) by Sir Henry W. A. Deterding and donated by him in the
same year to the Mauritshuis. There are several replicas or copies.

REMBRANDT VAN RIJN (1606–1669)

THE COMPANY OF FRANS BANNINGH COCQ
(THE NIGHTWATCH)   Canvas
Rijksmuseum No. 2016   Height 359 cm. (141³/₈″)
                        Width 438 cm. (172¹/₂″)

In 1638 Marie de Medici paid a visit to the town
of Amsterdam, the first queen to come to the
Republic of the United Netherlands. The Queen
was received with great ceremony. The companies
of the Civic Guard lined the streets through which
she passed. After this visit the town commissioned
a number of artists to commemorate the event. It
may have been on this occasion that Rembrandt
was commissioned to paint the company com-
manded by Frans Cocq. It was to be a large
canvas to decorate the long wall of the Hall of
the Civic Guard on Doelenstraat. Rembrandt was
given the left part of the wall, the centre part
being reserved for Nicolaes Elias, and the right
for a similar panel Jacob Backer.

In the centre of *The Nightwatch* Captain
Banningh Cocq gives the order to march to his
lieutenant, Willem van Ruytenburgh. On the far
right the drum beats. Several guardsmen pick up
their lances which are leaning against the wall.
Others, in the centre, like the man in red, recharge
their arms. Behind him the ensign Jan Visscher
Cornelissen flourishes his flag. On the left, Sergeant
Reynier Engelen is seated on a low wall, a pike
in his hand, Rombout Kemp is standing on the
right, talking, his arm outstretched. Two small
girls in pale dresses give light touches to the heavy
tones.

To its dominant obscurity the picture owes its
common but incorrect title *The Nightwatch*. It seems
that we should visualise, not a night scene but a nar-
row shaded street lit by a few rays of sunshine – perhaps the Doelenstraat.

Rembrandt finished this work in 1672. Until 1715 it was in the large
hall of the Kloveniersdoelen. It was later placed in the small chamber of

184

the Council of War. It is thought that it was then shortened on the left and slightly on the other sides. *The Nightwatch* was transferred to the Rijksmuseum, at first to the Trippenhuis and in 1885 to the present building.

REMBRANDT VAN RIJN (1606–1669)

TOBIT AND ANNA WITH THE HE-GOAT

Rijksmuseum No. 2024 A 12

Panel

Height 39.5 cm. (15⁵/₈″)

Width 30 cm. (11³/₄″)

The panel with the story of Tobit and the little goat is dated 1626. It is the earliest work by Rembrandt to be seen in a Dutch museum. The story shown here is in the Apocrypha (Tobit, 2:13 – 3:6). Anna, wife of old blind Tobit has been paid for her wool spinning and given a little goat. When she comes home with it and the old man hears the animal bleating, he thinks she has stolen it. He refuses to believe her explanation that it was a present and, desperate at the thought that his wife has sinned, prays to the Lord that he may die rather than hear false words.

The subject and the composition of the scene were not an original idea of Rembrandt's. He copied the scene from a print by Jan van de Velde, made after a drawing by Willem Buytenwech, making scarcely any changes at all. Some parts of this early work are unprecedented in their excellence of painting, for instance, the subtly elaborated grey-brown fur lining of Tobias' worn pink gown and the folded hands of the old man. But the piece also contains weak spots from which it can be seen that the artist had not reached full maturity yet. The action of the two figures is very theatrical; the space of the little room in which the performance – for that is really what it is – is enacted is improbably narrow and the artist does not make it clear to the viewer how the hut, which seems over-full with all kinds of domestic utensils and Anna's spinning gear and in which the fire seems to be placed directly on the stone floor, is arranged. The rendering of the various elements is intensely detailed, in accordance with the custom of the Leyden school of painting. Whereas his companion Gerard Dou was later to achieve even greater refinement in this direction, Rembrandt abandoned this technique after he had left Leyden. The broad touch and the mystical combination of light and dark for which the painter became famous are scarcely present here. That, too, he was only to develop in his Amsterdam period. The story of Tobit gripped Rembrandt throughout his life. In 1645 he repeated the story of the little goat; in 1659 he was to paint the old couple again, waiting for the return of their son, and he also devoted etchings and drawings to this story.

The painting comes from the Tschugin Collection in Moscow and later went into that of Dr H Baron Thyssen Bornemisza of Lugano. Baroness Bentinck née Baroness Thyssen Bornemisza of London lent it to the Rijksmuseum in 1956.

186

REMBRANDT VAN RIJN (1606–1669)
THE STONE BRIDGE   Panel
Rijksmuseum No. 2020   Height 29.5 cm. (11¹/₂")
                                            Width 42.5 cm. (16⁵/₈")

In the years when he lived in Amsterdam Rembrandt roamed about a lot
in the surroundings of the city, armed with his sketchbook and drawing
pen. The landscape with the stone bridge, painted in the late afternoon,
was the result of one those excursions. The sun, already low in the west,
plays on leaves and road while dark clouds gather in the east foreboding
bad weather. They make the small panel into a captivating play of light
and dark. The landscape must have been painted in 1637 or 1638. It
comes from the collections of Lapeyrière (Paris, 1817), James Gray (Ver-
sailles, 1863) and the Marquis of Lansdowne (Bowood, 1883). Bought by
the Rijksmuseum at the sale of James Reiss of London in 1900 with con-
tributions by the Rembrandt Society and Dr A. Bredius.

REMBRANDT VAN RIJN (1606–1669)
LAUGHING SELF-PORTRAIT   Copper
Mauritshuis No. 598   Height 15.4 cm. (6")
                                               Width 12.2 cm. (4⁷/₈")

There have been few painters of laughter. The fixing of that one moment
of gaiety which transforms the face is among the most difficult tasks.
Rembrandt dared it, and was successful. The painter wears an iron collar
as if he were a soldier, why is not known. He often portrayed himself and
others in disguises.

About 1629/1630. From the auctions of Van Cleef (Paris, 2nd April
1864), C. de Boissière (Paris, 19th February 1883) and the Langlois
Collection, Paris. Bought in Paris by the Mauritshuis in 1895.

REMBRANDT VAN RIJN (1606–1669)

SUSANNA BATHING
Mauritshuis No. 147

Panel

Height 47.5 cm. (18³/₄″).
Width 39 cm. (15³/₈″)

Anxiously Susanna turns away, hiding her nakedness as well as possible. Beautiful in the classical sense of the word she is not, and we know that Rembrandt was criticised for this reason by those among his contemporaries who advocated the ideal of classical beauty. They wished to see a naked figure as an ancient Venus statue, but Rembrandt, never having been in Italy and knowing the Greeks and Romans only from books and pictures and being little impressed by them, was of a different mind. To him the story of the chaste Susanna was not an excuse for displaying the splendid ideals of beauty held by antiquity, but a pathetic human case.

The story of Susanna was a cherished theme among the painters of the Baroque. Unedifying as it is, it does not apear in the Bible but at the end of the Old Testament Book of Daniel (Daniel 13) which is counted among the Apocrypha. In it one reads that Susanna lived in Babylon and was the wife of the wealthy Joachim. As she went bathing one day in the court of her house, having sent away her maids to get ointment and soap, she was surprised by two old men.

Contrary to most painters, who portrayed Susanna in her full beauty, still unaware of the disaster awaiting her, Rembrandt chose the moment in which she became aware of the watchers and cowered away in her fright. Not the beautiful picture that the old men saw before them with their covetous eyes, but the reaction of the suddenly surprised woman innocent of any evil. The beautiful clothes lying beside her, the golden ointment pot on the edge of the well, which is handsomely decorated with lobe ornaments in relief, and the stately palaces of Babylon in the background are indications of the environment in which the drama unfolded.

The date on the panel (enlarged on the right) should perhaps be read as 1637. The painting is from the auction of P. J. Snijders (Antwerp, 23rd May 1758) and from the collection of Govert van Slingelandt. In 1770 it was bought by Prince William V and with his collection it came to the Mauritshuis.

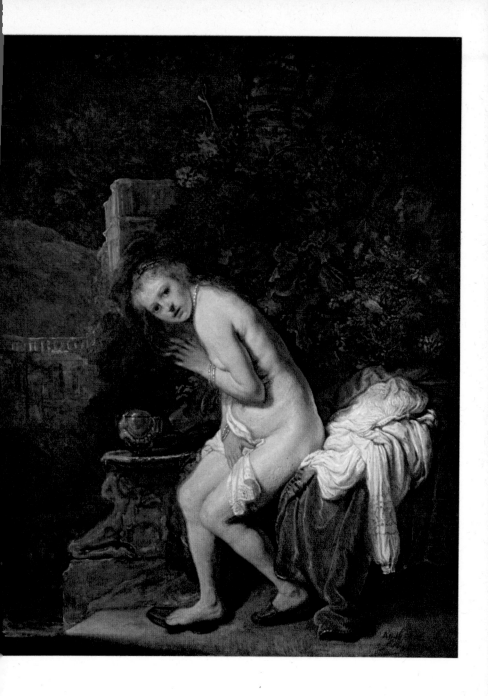

REMBRANDT VAN RIJN (1606–1669)

PORTRAIT OF REMBRANDT'S SON TITUS   Canvas

Boymans-van Beuningen Museum No. 381   Height 77 cm. (30¼″)

Width 63 cm. (24¾″)

This is how Rembrandt saw his thirteen-year-old son sitting, a small boy huddled behind a wooden desk too high for him, the ink well in an opened leather bag dangling between the fingers of the left hand, the quill-pen in the right hand while he presses his thumb against his soft child's cheek and stares before him, pondering over what he will put on paper. On the brown-blond curly locks lies a warmly-coloured beret. A somewhat brooding obscurity reigns over the room but bright light falls on the child. How different from Jan van Scorel's clear portrait of the sprightly, perhaps somewhat precocious, schoolboy (page 111) is this young Titus staring dreamily ahead of him. Yet here is the same theme, although treated in a totally different manner. Indeed, like Scorel, Rembrandt had been taught Latin in his younger years and like him he had come to know the spirit of Humanism, but in 1655, when his son sat for him, that was a long time ago. At this period artists were not concerned to display their learning; they were interested in a humanistic motif only in so far as it provided material for a purely pictorial creation and an interpretation of deep human feelings.

Rembrandt remained in the grip of the subject. About a year later he was to paint Titus again, reading a book, again with the beret on the exuberant curly hair, lit by a single sunray which gleams through the dimness of the room (Kunsthistorisches Museum, Vienna). This portrait of young Titus comes from the collection of the Earl of Crawford and Balcarres, London. It was bought by the Foundation of the Boymans Museum in 1940.

REMBRANDT VAN RIJN (1606–1669)

SAUL LISTENING TO DAVID PLAYING ON THE HARP   Canvas
Mauritshuis No. 621   Height 130.5 cm. (51¼″)
                                                        Width 164   cm. (64⅝″)

'And it came to pass, when the evil spirit from God was upon Saul. that David took an harp, and played with his hand: so Saul was refreshed, and was well, and the evil spirit departed from him' (I Samuel 16:23). This is the theme which inspired Rembrandt to one of his most impressive paintings. There sits the great king in grandiose attire, a gold crown on the colossal turban which marks him as an Oriental, the red velvet cloak of majesty round his shoulders over an exquisite golden yellow caftan; he holds a large javelin. Opposite him, as though huddled away in a corner in the semi-darkness, David, the humble Jewish boy, plays the harp. A few rays of light brush his face, neck and hands. The king is, of course, seated in the full light but is partly hidden by the curtain which hangs down the centre of the composition, separating the two figures; he is ashamed of the evil spirit which had taken possession of him and which he had not resisted and of the evil he has wrought; he hides his face in the drapery which must be attached to the canopy above the throne and with part of it wipes away a tear – a sign that he is beginning to recover.

Rembrandt, of course, did not paint this picture after a reading of only the sentence quoted. On the canvas appear details from other parts of the same story. There is the javelin in the hands of the monarch (its point is visible). I Samuel 18:10 and 11 tell of this terrible weapon with which Saul threatened David. This explains why the young harp-player sits so anxiously in his corner, his face turned away from his king, and why Saul hides his face from him: 'And Saul was afraid of David' (I Samuel 18:12).

Rembrandt neither signed nor dated the painting but it must belong to his mature period. For whom it was painted is not known. The earliest mention only dates from July 1826 when it was bought at the sale of A. J. Petit of Malines by Pieretz. Next it formed part of the sale of the Duke de Caraman (Paris, 10th May 1830), the Didot Collection in Paris and the Alphonse Oudry sale (Paris, 16th April 1869) where it was bought by Durand-Ruel. Thereafter it belonged to the collections of Arthur Stevens and Baron d'Oppenheim of Cologne who sold it to Bourgeois. He sold it to Georges d'Ay at Epernay, after which Durand-Ruel bought it back. Dr A. Bredius bought the canvas from him in 1898 at the Rembrandt Exhibition in Amsterdam, lent it to the Mauritshuis and bequeathed it to this institution on his death in 1946.

REMBRANDT VAN RIJN (1606–1669)
The Governors of the Cloth Guild (the Syndics)   Canvas
Rijksmuseum No. 2017   Height 191.5 cm.   (75½")
                                             Width 279   cm. (109⅞")

Curiously, until a short time ago it was not known who were depicted
in this world-famous painting. Only in 1957 did Miss I. H. van Eeghen
succeed, thanks to extensive knowledge of Amsterdam's municipal history
and much research, in ending the anonymity of the six figures shown. The
big canvas unofficially called *The Staalmeesters* or *Syndics* was painted in
1662 for the Wardens' chamber in the Clothiers' Guild in Amsterdam, where
there were six similar pieces hanging, each showing five seated gentlemen and one standing. The oldest dated from 1559. Rembrandt's commission entailed his following an established tradition. The College of
Syndics comprised, firstly, the cloth-dyer Willem or Gulliaam van Doeyen-
burg who was about forty-six years old (died 1687); in the painting he
occupies the Chairman's seat behind the centre of the table. The gentleman
on his left, who rises from his chair, is Volckert Jansz (died 1681). He
belonged to a Friesian Baptist family and in his leisure collected curios,
books and other interesting material. The oldest member of the company,
seated on the left, was Jacob van Loon (1585–1674), a Roman Catholic
who had a draper's shop in The Dam at the corner of the Kalverstraat.
On the extreme right sits another Catholic member of the College, Aernout
van der Mye (c. 1625–1681). He was a clothier in the Nieuwedijk and a
prominent personality in the cloth trade. The youngest Syndic, on the
right of the Chairman, is Jochem de Neve (1629–1681) who came from
a family with Nonconformist sympathies so that he could not make much
headway in the ruling world to which he belonged by birth.

Behind the gentlemen stands a sixth figure, the valet. By tradition he
was entitled to figure on the group-portrait of his masters. He did not
have to pay for this, but had to stand and remove his hat which his
masters never did in the badly heated houses of the time. Even in church
a gentleman did not take off his hat except during prayers. The old tradition of the valet appearing in the portrait of his masters has not yet
fallen into disuse in the Netherlands.

Six different types, very divergent characters judging by their faces,
members of different religions who in the free Republic could live beside
and with one another, are here grouped around a table. The modest black
and white of their clothes contrasts with the costly red Eastern cloth on
the table which gleams in the ray of sunlight falling into the room. The

group, on whose composition Rembrandt spent extreme care, is held together, as it were, by the oak panelling of the rear wall which protrudes a little on either side. On the right one sees about two thirds of the chimney piece; on the left, part of the side wall in which the windows are set.

The painting was placed in the Syndics' Court in Amsterdam in 1662 and was transferred on 27th November 1771 to the art room of the town hall. Since 15th August 1808 it has been lent to the State by the city of Amsterdam.

REMBRANDT VAN RIJN (1606–1669)

SELF-PORTRAIT AS THE APOSTLE PAUL

Rijksmuseum No. 2024 A 13

Canvas

Height 91 cm. (35⁷/₈″)

Width 77 cm. (30¹/₄″)

In about 1661 Rembrandt painted a number of apostles and evangelists. Whether they made up a series, and whether this was ever finished, we can no longer establish. Several of these canvases have been preserved until the present day, scattered over the whole world, but they no longer constitute a complete set. It is assumed that Rembrandt's *Self-portrait as the Apostle Paul* formed part of this sequence. The figure has the customary attributes of Paul, a sword and a book. Curiously enough, he wears the sword under his left armpit instead of at his side. But the Biblical attributes usually matter little to whoever looks at it; what he sees is a monumental, striking self-portrait, one of the last of the long and varied series in which the artist immortalized his own features. Here he is revealed as an old man; at fifty-five he is grey-haired and worn with age.

Underneath the signature, the canvas carries the date 1661 to the left of the centre. It originated in the year, therefore, when Rembrandt painted the *Claudius Civilis* for the new Amsterdam town hall, the big canvas which was removed shortly after it had been put in position. It is the disappointment over this calamity which shows on the painters face? He had had to swallow even more before that. A few years previously he had been declared bankrupt. His beautiful house and precious art-treasures had been sold. For a long time, already, domestic worries had borne heavily on him. Should the expression of his face be interpreted as the wise resignation of a man purified by sorrow? Or is it more correct to restrict oneself to establishing that suffering and tragedy marked this face? We can only guess.

The painting belonged successively to the collections of Fournier in Paris and Corsini in Rome (until 1807). After that it belonged to Lord Kinnaird, Rossie Priory, near Dundee. Next it was acquired by Mr and Mrs De Bruyn - van der Leeuw of Muri. In 1959 Mrs de Bruyn donated it to the Rijksmuseum.

REMBRANDT VAN RIJN
(1606–1669)

THE BRIDAL COUPLE

(THE JEWISH BRIDE)　　　　Canvas

Rijksmuseum No. 2019

Height 121.5 cm. (47⅞″)

Width　166.5 cm. (65½″)

Nothing is known of the early history of this painting. It is mentioned for the first time as being sold by a Mr Vaillant of Amsterdam to the London art dealer J. Smith in 1825, and it has always carried the traditional title. It is of course quite possible that the two figures portrayed are indeed Jews but the word 'bride' should be approached with some caution. It has been suggested that Rembrandt was portraying a biblical scene here, an illustration of Genesis 38:14–18, the story of Judah and Thamar.

A verbal description is quite inadequate to do the work full justice—its sober composition concentrating on the two figures whilst the background is only indicated sketchily; the timorous gesture of the three majestically-painted hands; the beautiful, thickly laid on colours of the clothes, varying from a soft salmon colour to brilliant canary yellow (all this fairly light in tone since the canvas was cleaned in 1960); the profusion of pearls and other jewellery.

The Jewish Bride is from Rembrandt's last period and probably originated after 1665. From 1833 it was part of the collection of A. van der Hoop of Amsterdam who bequeathed it to the city in 1854. In 1885 the city lent it to the Rijsmuseum.

200

HERCULES PIETERSZ SEGHERS (1589 or 1590–1637 or 1638)

LANDSCAPE
Boymans-van Beuningen Museum

Canvas on Panel
Height 29.2 cm. (11¹/₂″)
Width 54.5 cm. (21¹/₂″)

When this unsigned painting turned up in England at the Sotheby sale in London on 9th May 1951, it was announced as being by the hand of Jan de Vos (1593–1649). Though incorrect, this was a likely attribution. The Leyden artist Jan de Vos had been a contemporary of Seghers and did indeed work in the same style. Through the art dealer D. A. Hoogendijk of Amsterdam the work was subsequently acquired by the Boymans Museum after having been identified as a masterpiece by Seghers.

The wide landscape and the way in which it is composed, with a mountain and coppice in the foreground and beyond that a vista of trees and some buildings, do not differ from the conception of landscape art prevalent during that period in most towns of the provinces of Holland and Utrecht. The working out of this theme here is much more arresting, however, than with the popular masters of the period such as Esaias and Jan van de Velde, Alexander Keirinx or Gilles d'Hondecoeter. How much grander is Seghers' work 'bound together by the warm light of late afternoon which makes the colours of nature darker, banishes the fleeting shadows and tender nuances, and evokes a static and yet radiant universe, like a moonscape' (J. G. van Gelder). There is no point in trying to identify the landscape, for it has been built up from elements which may have existed separately but which only came together in the imagination of the artist. The view stretched over the flat land of Holland, with a hilly horizon which, like the hill covered with vegetation in the foreground, reminds one of the Montferland or the Elterberg in the province of Gelderland; in the middle, a small pool which may have been inspired by a backwater of the Rhine in the same area; all this is filled out with a rotunda, which seems to come from Italy, and a square tower standing by itself, a favourite motif of Seghers which he painted on two more of his sketches. But on further consideration the view appears to be too wide after all to be typically Dutch. It reminds us that Seghers must have travelled through mountainous regions where he would have had the opportunity of seeing below him wide plains spread out at his feet.

The landscape in the Boymans-van Beuningen Museum appears to be a late work by Seghers; perhaps it originated about 1630–1632.

CAREL FABRITIUS (1622–1654)

Self-portrait
Boymans-van Beuningen Museum No. 139

Panel
Height 65 cm. (25⁵/₈")
Width 49 cm. (19¹/₄")

The Fabritius brothers both painted two self-portraits. Those by Barend, and that by Carel in Munich recall Rembrandt in method and treatment. The artists wear handsome clothes, like those of Rembrandt in his self-portraits, with dashing caps on their curly locks and cloaks flung loosely over their shoulders. The other self-portrait of Carel Fabritius, in Rotterdam, is hatless and without theatricality, or any attempt to show the model as handsomer than he was; it is direct, true-to-life and original. Bequeathed to the Museum by F. J. O. Boymans in 1847.

CAREL FABRITIUS (1622–1654)
THE GOLDFINCH   Panel
Mauritshuis No. 605   Height 33.7 cm. (13¹/₄″)
                                                 Width 22.6 cm.   (8⁷/₈″)

The Goldfinch is unique in the history of painting. Until recently the
manner, subject and inspiration remained unclassifiable. Only in 1950 did
a young Swedish art-historian, Kjell Boström, show that the panel had
been a door for a niche decorated in trompe-l'oeil, a genre in which Fabritius excelled. Often they were designed to cover a fireplace in summer
when it was not in use. They were, of course, not framed; this would have
disturbed the illusion. In the Arenberg, Camberlyn, Thore-Bürger and
Martinet sales; bought at the latter by the Mauritshuis in 1896.

FERDINAND BOL (1616–1680)
PORTRAIT OF BOY IN POLISH COSTUME — Canvas
Boymans-van Beuningen Museum No. 48 — Height 158.5 cm. (62¹/₄″)
Width 120.5 cm. (47¹/₂″)

Why is the boy dressed so exotically? We know only that Polish attire was
popular in the Netherlands in the seventeenth century, Bol's master Rembrandt used it, for instance, in *The Polish Horseman*. The enthusiastically
received visit of Queen Louise Maria Gonzaga to Amsterdam in 1645, on
her way to Poland, may have given rise to this fashion. Bol's portrait of this
still unidentified boy is as charming as it is elegant. It is dated 1656; the
Van der Waeyen coat-of-arms was added in the nineteenth century. Bought
by the Rotterdam Museum in 1865.

206

NICOLAES MAES (1634–1693)
<small>DREAMING</small>   Canvas
Rijksmuseum No. 1502   Height 123 cm. (48³/₈″)
                                        Width   96 cm. (37³/₄″)

Nicolaes Maes had been back about two years in his native town of
Dordrecht, away from the guidance of his great master Rembrandt but
still strongly influenced by his art, when in about 1655 he painted this
young woman. She is simply dressed, perhaps a servant or peasant. The
subject recalls Rembrandt though the concept of the figure is less profound,
the brushwork less heavy. Maes was to turn slowly away from the example
of Rembrandt to the lighter style of the next generation. The painting is
from Groningen and was bought by the Rijksmuseum in 1829.

AERT DE GELDER (1645–1727)
PORTRAIT OF ERNST VAN BEVEREN   Canvas
Rijksmuseum No. 966 B 6   Height 128 cm. (50³/₈")
                                              Width   105 cm. (41³/₈")

In his portraits Rembrandt often worked in a realistic manner but sometimes he dressed up his models in strange costumes, which create a splendid
effect but impress to-day's viewer as resembling a weird fancy-dress party.
His example was followed by many of his pupils. Aert de Gelder here shows
the ruler Ernst van Beveren, Lord of West-IJsselmonde and de Linde,
Sheriff and subsequently Mayor of the venerable town of Dordrecht, in
fancy-dress. He wears a doublet of a cut no longer in fashion in 1685
– the date appearing on the canvas – but considered to be 'Burgundian'
that is, reminscent of the 'old fatherland'. It most nearly resembled early
sixteenth-century wear. Over the doublet is a heavy grey-green, red-lined
coat embroidered with gold thread and fastened with cords, highly decorative, but scarcely wearable as an article ever of formal apparel, unless on
the stage. This heavy coat harmonises wonderfully with the woven cloth
with green leaves which covers the table in the lower right hand corner.
A curtain in the right upper corner completes the composition. It has been
partly opened to disclose a cupboard with books. In comparison with its
height the canvas is remarkably wide so that it is well adopted to the
broad figure. The portrait is one of De Gelder's most impressive works.
   Ernst van Beveren was born in 1659 and was therefore about twenty-six
years old when he was painted in this self-assured and ostentatious pose.
A family coat of arms which was later added to the top left corner of the
canvas disappeared during recent cleaning. The portrait came, presumably
by inheritance, into the possession of Baron van Hardenbroek van Berg-
ambacht of The Hague. At a sale in Amsterdam in 1918 it was bought by
the collector J. J. M. Chabot of Wassenaar (later of Clarens). After his
death and as a result of the Second World War it came to the State which
lent it in 1946 to the Rijksmuseum.

PHILIPS DE KONINCK (1619–1688)

VIEW OVER A FLAT LANDSCAPE   Canvas
Boymans-van Beuningen Museum No. 243   Height   95 cm. (37³/₈")
                                       Width   120 cm. (47¹/₄")

Extensive landscapes riven by streams, evocations of wide space under high, cloud-burdened skies – these were the specialities of Philips de Koninck. These views often seem to have been taken from the Elterberg, the Swan Tower in Cleve or the Valkhof in Nijmegen, but after further consideration they all appear to be fantasies on the theme of the Rhenish plain, studded with farms or elegant country-houses which do not really exist in that neighbourhood, with parties of hunters, travellers or dream-towns which recall Arnhem in the distance. In them reality is improved and embellished.

Philips de Koninck was born in Amsterdam, the son of a well-to-do goldsmith, Aert de Koninck. He received his artistic training from his elder brother Jacob at Rotterdam. In 1641 he returned to Amsterdam, the city in which he lived until his death. There he became friendly with Rembrandt and Vondel. The art of the first influenced his work while he portrayed the latter several times. Apart from being an artist Philips de Koninck also kept an inn at the Rotterdam ferry station and so was assured of a decent income. Was it on the ships which moored there that he undertook journeys, from a spontaneous urge for pure enjoyment of nature and in quest of subjects for his canvases? Curiously enough, we know hardly anything about this with certainty. It is noteworthy that the appearance of Amsterdam itself, of the canals and the river IJssel, does not seem to have held any attractions for this man although he lived in that city for almost the whole of his life. In this De Koninck may be compared with an artist like Meindert Hobbema, except that some of his drawings must have originated in the Dutch polder country right under the smoke of Amsterdam. They are reminiscent of the numerous topographically accurate sketches which Rembrandt made in the environs of the city.

This panoramic view over flat land is dated 1664. In 1847 it was bequeathed by F. J. O. Boymans to the museum at Rotterdam.

ADRIAEN VAN DE VELDE (1636–1672)

FAMILY GROUP IN A LANDSCAPE   Canvas
Rijksmuseum No. 2446   Height 148 cm. (58¼″)
                                     Width 178 cm. (70⅛″)

In the Renaissance the habit of travelling to the countryside and enjoying nature had arisen; in the Middle Ages this had not been the custom. Nature had been considered essentially as a source, provided by the Creator, of all kinds of useful materials such as grain, vegetables, meat, wool and anything else Man needed. That nature could also be beautiful and could provide relaxation they did not realise, at least not consciously.

The 'discovery' of nature led to the emergence of the country house, first of all in Italy; next this fashion gradually spread over the countries of Western Europe. For going into the country had rapidly become so popular that it may well be called a fashion. In Holland country places arose everywhere during the seventeenth century in the neighbourhood of the large towns. Hotels with 'holiday-accomodation' did not yet exist in those days. Not only did the well-to-do townsmen possess their country residences; before long it was no exception to find that the better-off middle classes, too, could afford a stay in the country during the summer.

Adriaen van de Velde was influenced by this new trend when he painted his landscape with family group. Or should one speak of a family portrait in a landscape? It is difficult to decide which to call it. Judging from the various features shown, the picture is of the edge of the sandy dunes west of Haarlem. It was in that town that the painter had enjoyed the most important part of his training, studying under Jan Wijnants and perhaps also Philips Wouwerman. The couple in the centre are possibly the artist himself and his wife. The head of this man should be compared with Van de Velde's self-portrait in the Municipal Museum at The Hague. In 1667 – the date appearing on the great landscape – he was thirty-one years old, which may well correspond with the age of the gentleman in the picture. The colours of the figures, especially of the lady's red frock, that of the maid with the child on her lap on the left, and of the two white horses before the open cart in the background, are fresh and contrastingly piquant against the more subdued tones of the landscape. These elements give the broadly-treated whole highlights of spontaneous gaiety. It is a painting in which all reserve, complexity and heaviness have been overcome. We do not know if the building which sticks out in the distance above the trees was a country house owned by Adriaen van de Velde, or whether he had perhaps only rented it for the duration of a summer.

The painting comes from the sales of Lord Rendlesham (London, 1806) and J. van der Pals (Rotterdam, 1824). The Amsterdam collector A. van der Hoop bought it in 1834 in London from J. Nieuwenhuys. In 1854 he bequeathed it to the city of Amsterdam which in 1885 lent it to the Rijksmuseum.

JACOB ISAACKSZ VAN RUISDAEL (1628 or 1629–1682)

VIEW OF HAARLEM   Canvas
Rijksmuseum No. 2071   Height 43 cm. (16⅞")
                                    Width 38 cm. (15")

Ruisdael painted Haarlem dozens of times, most often seen from the west, where the first row of dunes near Overgeen gave him a wide panorama. Perhaps it was his patrons who made the painter repeat the same theme so often.

Ruisdael's views of Haarlem are not all the same shape. Some are broad so as to leave room for portraying the surroundings; others are tall, three-quarters filled by grey, cloud-laden sky, with the silhouette of the town in the background. It seems that such wide vistas must have been more to the artist than just a picturesque point of departure. In this view of Haarlem which hangs in the Boston Museum there is the small castle at Cleve where in 1573 the Spanish Commander Don Federico de Toledo established his headquarters during the notorious siege of Haarlem. But we know that the castle was in ruins in Ruisdael's time, which proves that he was interested in historical as well as picturesque themes. Is this also true of the picture in the Rijksmuseum? We cannot tell. But Ruisdael was certainly interested in other things besides the picturesque and colour. For example the linen in the foreground; we know that Haarlem's surroundings were renowned for their bleaching-establishments.

The painting dates from 1670. It comes from the sale of Baron van Nagell van Ampsen (The Hague, 1851). Bequeathed to the Rijksmuseum in 1870 by L. Dupper Wzn of Dordrecht.

MEINDERT HOBBEMA (1638–1709)
A WATER-MILL   Panel
Rijksmuseum No. 1188
Height 62   cm. (24³/₈″)
Width   85.5 cm. (33³/₄″)

Hobbema is both a disciple of the classical landscapists, such as Ruisdael, and an
innovator in this genre. Although he
lived in Amsterdam he often went into
the country to find his landscape-
subjects. He was inspired by the dunes
of the North Sea but preferred the
wooded parts of East-Gelderland and
Overijssel. In 1660 he had already visited
that region, in the company of his master
who had been there before. Whilst
Ruisdael's preference was for vistas
arrestingly lighted by a complicated
play of sun and shade, with trees serving
as foils, for Hobbema the trees form a
foreground which screens the horizon
from view. Ruisdael's favourite, dramatic
cloud masses and sombre shadows make
way for the serenity of a diffuse sunlight
and subtle nuances of colour. In this
Hobbema heralds the painting of the
eighteenth century.

The subject of *A Water-Mill* in the
Rijksmuseum was often used by Hobbema.
The painting came from the William
Smith Collection, London; was auctioned
in London in 1822; in Paris in 1824; in
London in 1831; in Edinburgh in 1835;
A. van der Hoop Collection, Amsterdam.
Bequeathed by him in 1854 to the city
of Amsterdam, which in 1885 lent it to
the Rijksmuseum.

WILLEM VAN DE VELDE THE YOUNGER (1633–1707)

THE CAPTURED PRIZES OF THE FOUR-DAY SEA BATTLE   Canvas

Rijksmuseum No. 2471   Height 58 cm. (22⁷/₈″)

Width 81 cm. (31⁷/₈″)

The navies of the Netherlands Republic and England fought each other in three wars in the seventeenth century (1652–1654, 1665–1667, 1672–1674). Of these wars we possess a rich heritage of paintings by Willem van de Velde the Elder, the son of a sea-captain. Sailing had been in his blood from an early age. When battle was joined he had the Admiral's express consent to sail round between the big ships in a galley, making accurate sketches of what occurred, like a press photographer of today. On his return home he elaborated these notes into the great pen and ink pictures. He cannot really be called a painter. His son worked differently. He had received his training from the naval painter Simon de Vlieger, but he used his father's drawings as a basis for his pictures. There appears to have been a division of labour between father and son which achieved exceedingly good results. As an exception, however, Van de Velde the Younger appears to have been present at the great Four-Day Battle (11th–14th June 1666) in which Admirals de Ruyter and Cornelis Tromp defeated the English Fleet under the Duke of Albermarle and Prince Rupert off the North Foreland. There is, at any rate, a drawing by his hand on which can be seen the capture of the English ship, the 'Royal Prince' which had got stuck on the Galloper sandbank. He also made two pictures of another episode of this engagement, the arrival at the Goereese Gat of the captured ships 'Seven Oaks', 'Royal George' and 'Convertine'. This event made a tremendous impression on Dutchmen which explains why this commemorative picture was commissioned. The Dutch red, white and blue flutters proudly from the escutcheons of the captured ships, which have been disarmed after their defeat, their sails full of holes. The picture is both an interesting and reliable historical document and an attractive work of art. The sea is calm. Sunrays from the high, half-clouded sky sparkle on the grey water and cast spots of light on the hulls and sails of some ships. This could almost be called 'open-air-painting'. It is as though one smells the salt sea wind, and the empty foreground gives an impression of breadth. The composition is skilful, the colours alive and real.

From the sales of J. P. Wierman (Amsterdam, 1762) and Neufville (Rotterdam, 1785). G. van der Pot Collection, Rotterdam; bought by the Rijksmuseum in 1808.

JAN VAN DER HEYDEN (1637–1712)
IMAGINARY VIEW OF THE CHURCH OF VEERE
Mauritshuis No. 815

Canvas

Height 31.5 cm. (12¹/₂″)
Width 36 cm. (14¹/₈″)

The artist was born at Gorkum but lived for the greater part of his life in Amsterdam. He travelled, once visiting Veere in Zeeland, a small town with a crowded past. During the fifteenth and sixteenth centuries the Netherlandish navy achored in its harbour. From those great days dated the Church of Our Lady with its monumental tower, painted true-to-life by Van der Heyden; its environs spring from his imagination.

In the evening sun the shadows have grown long. A few figures enliven the scene, but without disturbing the quietness of the atmosphere.

From the Blumenthal Collection, Paris. Then in the sale of L. Cottereau (Paris, 30th May 1870). Bought by the Mauritshuis in 1935.

GERRIT ADRIAENSZOON BERCKHEYDE (1638–1698)

The Great Market at Haarlem   Canvas

Frans Hals Museum No. 464 a   Height 69.5 cm. (27¹/₄″)

Width 90.5 cm. (35⁵/₈″)

In contrast to Jan van der Heyden's imaginary view of the Church of Veere, the cool, clear view of the Great Market at Haarlem by his contemporary Gerrit Berckheyde is a purely 'realistic portrait' of a town. It raises no problems; it is a very accurate, if rather cold, reproduction of a part of Haarlem.

The painting is dated 1696. Lent by the Rijksdienst Roorende Kunstberit at The Hague.

WILLEM CLAESZOON HEDA (1594–1680)
STILL LIFE Panel
Frans Hals Museum No. 705 Height 58.5 cm. (23")
Width 79 cm. (31¹/₈")

A still-life with one or two jugs, a few glasses, a plate, a dish with a pie
or half a dozen oysters beside which lies a lemon, has long been called a
'breakfast-piece' by art historians. This term should not, however, be
understood to mean that our ancestors of the seventeenth century started
their day with a meal of pies or oysters and beer or wine. The original
meaning of the term 'breakfast' was 'a light meal at any hour of the
day', and it was more often used to mean 'everything set out for a meal,
including the food, cutlery and crockery'. Haarlem was the town where
the art of painting breakfast-pieces was most practised and achieved its
most beautiful results. The greatest master in this field was Willem Claes-
zoon Heda. Especially in the first half of the seventeenth century,
Dutchmen did not limit themselves to painting the dishes, pitchers, glasses
and food with careful realism; they liked to philosophise on what they
saw, to make their still-lifes teach a moral. To them food and drink became
symbols of the transitory nature of material things. The same was true of
glass, while precious metals aroused associations of riches which in the
hereafter would be valueless. It is not possible to define accurately to what
extend Heda wished to perpetuate such thoughts symbolically in his still-
lifes but it is certain that he worked them into his paintings.

Heda's breakfast-piece in the Frans Hals Museum is light in touch and
very soft in tone, with tender grey silver and pewter – how refined is the
difference in appearance between these two metals! – and white table
damask, verging on grey. The knife which cut the pie has a handsome
handle inlaid with mother-of-pearl; on the blade one reads in small, modest
but clear lettering the signature of the painter and the date: HEDA 1633.

Bought in 1957 from an Amsterdam art-dealer with the help of the
Rembrandt Society.

WILLEM KALF (1619–1693)

STILL LIFE

Rijksmuseum No. 1320

Canvas
Width 62 cm. (24³/₈")
Height 71.5 cm. (28¹/₂")

At the head of the long list of Northern-Netherlandish still-life painters
– in the seventeenth century alone there were more than five hundred –
stands the name of Willem Kalf. His first teacher was Cornelis Saftleven,
who taught him how to paint gentle interiors with peasants, cooks, vegetables and all kinds of utensils. We do not know what his second master, the
many-sided Hendrick Gerritsz Pot of Haarlem, added to Kalf's knowledge
and concepts. Later, between 1640 and 1645, we find him in Paris among
the large circle of 'Flemish' artists who made a good living there. Kalf's
palette became softer here and his interest turned more and more to in-
animate objects. He was influenced by the Southern-Netherlandish painter
François Rijckhals but his first still-lifes were not of very high quality.
Only after he returned to Amsterdam did he achieve full mastery of the
style which made him famous. Kalf turned to chiaroscuro painting, possibly under the influence of Rembrandt. Like him, he also entered the art-
trade (note the quantities of Oriental carpets, Chinese porcelain and exquisite silverwork in his still-lifes). The painting in the Rijksmuseum belongs to the group of exquisite still-lifes in which Kalf rendered the riches
of Holland, looming up from the almost mystical obscurity of an un-
clearly defined room. The portrayal of the material is perfect; the fine
Chinese Ming dish, the richly decorated, typically Dutch silver jug and
the fragile glass have been arranged with great feeling for harmony.
Amidst all this richness the artist retained a certain reserve, however, which
resulted in delicacy rather than pompousness. Often the artist used the
same object in more than one composition, but the groupings varied
according to his fancy at the time. The Sans Souci Palace near Potsdam
possessed a still-life by Kalf very like the one in the Rijksmuseum. The
piece was acquired for the museum in 1821 at the sale of the A. J. Brandt
Collection.

224

JAN DAVIDSZ DE HEEM (1606–1683 or 1684)

STILL LIFE

Boymans-van Beuningen Museum No. 184

Canvas

Height 75 cm. (29¹/₂″)
Width 105 cm. (41³/₈″)

Jan Davidsz de Heem had a long way to go before achieving mastery of
the style by which he was to become known. He began with breakfast-
pieces in the Haarlem style. After moving to Leyden he became interested
in the 'vanitas' and still-lifes with books. But when he was thirty years
old, he became acquainted in Antwerp with the *pronk* still-life and devoted
the rest of his life to painting such works. Yet he never entirely became
a Southern-Netherlander. He toned down the Flemish excesses in his compositions by carefully chosen, even lighting which blended objects of many
differing sorts and colours into one harmonic whole. In later years De
Heem now and then returned to the North Netherlands. There he became
the driving force behind a development and popularization of the Antwerp
manner of still-life painting.

This painting was acquired in 1865 by the Rotterdam Museum.

ABRAHAM VAN BEYEREN (1620 or 1621–1690)
STILL LIFE   Canvas
Rijksmuseum No. 505 A 3   Height 126 cm. (49⅝")
                                                          Width 106 cm. (41¾")

Again and again Abraham van Beyeren was forced to move, persecuted
by his creditors. It seems curious that this artist, constantly in financial
difficulties, excelled in the depiction of sumptuous *pronk* still-lifes. Silverwork and gold, watches and jewellery, porcelain, fine glass, velvet carpets,
exotic fruit and flowers are heaped together on marble table-tops. In the
soft light of his studio the wine glitters in a goblet, while a piece of silver
shines from the semi-obscurity. This delicate still-life with its light touch
must date from about 1655. In 1958 it was bought by the Rijksmuseum.

227

ABRAHAM VAN BEYEREN (1620 or 1621–1690)
STILL LIFE WITH FISH   Panel
Frans Hals Museum No. 724   Height 46.5 cm. (57⁵/₈″)
                                             Width 64   cm. (25¹/₄″)

Fish, one of the sources of Dutch prosperity in the Golden Age, was a
favourite subject with many Dutch artists, including Abraham van Beyeren.
As the son of a glass-maker of The Hague he must in his youth have seen
newly-caught fish on the Scheveningen beach. He probably started painting
it under the influence of his brother-in-law and teacher, Pieter de Putter.
That Van Beyeren had contacts with the fishing trade appears from the
great plaque in the Church of Maassluis which the fishing guild of that
town ordered from him. Moreover he often painted from a small boat.

   This picture is realistic and baroque in composition. Another version,
with a few differences, hangs in the University Museum at Lund.

   Bought in 1959 from the Haarlem art-market.

ADRIAEN VAN OSTADE (1610–1684)

THE FISH VENDOR   Canvas

Rijksmuseum No. 1820 A 2   Height 36.5 cm. (14¹/₄″)
                                                 Width   39.5 cm. (15¹/₂″)

After the fish, the fishwife ... She is from Haarlem, like Ostade, who
devoted himself to painting humble people. According to Houbraken he
took lessons from Frans Hals but the latter's influence is not apparent in
his work. But the stay at Haarlem of Adriaen Brouwer, a worthy successor
to Brueghel, in 1627, must have meant a great deal to the young artist.
The canvas is dated 1672. A variant is in the Budapest Museum. From the
sales of Gerard Braamcamp (Amsterdam, 1771) and P. de Smeth van Alphen
(Amsterdam, 1810). Six van Hillegom and J. Six Collections, Amsterdam.
Donated to the Rijksmuseum by Sir Henry Deterding in 1936.

AELBERT CUYP (1620–1691)

PIETER DE ROOVERE DIRECTING THE SALMON FISHING NEAR DORDRECHT

Canvas

Mauritshuis No. 25

Height 123 cm. (48¹/₂″)

Width 154 cm. (60⁵/₈″)

This is a portrait of the Dordrecht aristocrat Pieter de Roovere, (son of Pompejus) Lord of Hardinxveld (1602–1658), who was Bailiff of South Holland. The identification of the figure is based on the family coat-of-arms which hangs on the front of the horse's harness and a comparison with another portrait of Lord Pieter which is preserved in Dordrecht. The painting may have originated a few years before the death of the sitter, in about 1650 when Aelbert Cuyp was about thirty years old. The fisherman to the right holds out a salmon; other fish lie on the ground, indicating, with the water and the fishermen behind, that De Roovere was in charge of salmon fishing on the river near Dordrecht. In the seventeenth century salmon fishing was an important source of income for Dordrecht. The house in the background recalls the fact that the island of Dordrecht used to be studded with country-residences where the well-to-do citizens passed the summer.

The velvet, fur-lined costume of the horseman is elegant and seems slightly fantastic. Did the inhabitants of Dordrecht actually wear such clothes in the middle of the seventeenth century? Certainly such pseudo-Polish (or Hungarian) costume was a caprice of fashion in those years, and appears in several portraits of the period (see page 206).

Through Aelbert Cuyp's talent this occasional piece became an attractive work of art no less than an interesting and representative scene. That the painting used to enjoy a certain popularity can be seen from the fact that there are several copies of it. Through inheritance the piece came into the possession of Jonkheer O. Repelaer van Driel (1759–1832) of Dordrecht, whose great-grandmother was a De Roovere. In 1820 it was bought from him by the Mauritshuis.

JAN HAVICKSZ STEEN (1626–1679)

The Inn   Canvas

Mauritshuis No. 170   Height 68 cm. (26³/₄″)
                                                  Width 82 cm. (32¹/₄″)

In order to protect their paintings against dust, seventeenth-century Dutch painters were accustomed to
hang a cloth over them when not actually working on
them. Often 'imitation' curtains were painted on the
canvas or panel itself as a form of *trompe-l'œil*. This
was particularly popular with Leyden painters, such
as Dou and Rembrandt, and Jan Steen, too, devoted
a good deal of time to them. The result can be seen
in the exquisite grey silk drapings which fill the top
part of his *Inn* at the Mauritshuis. It is a phenomenally
skilful rendering of material, airily draped so that the
light enhances its beauty and makes the rich qualities
of the silk glow even richer.

The curtain has nothing to do with the interior
painted below. It only serves as a foil giving the
necessary depth to the picture. Here are, together in
a spacious room, all the little subjects which Jan Steen
portrayed so often: the children playing happily, the
young, rosy-cheeked, healthy woman, the dandy, the
old fool in love, the players and drinkers, the table
with the precious Turkish rug and the still-life of
dishes, colourful fruit and fine glasswork, on which
the light sparkles, the oysters and broken eggs, the dog
and cat, the solid Dutch furniture and the painting
in the carved gilded frame on the wall. With all these
figures and objects *The Inn* has become one of Steen's
most elaborate works. Whether this is really an inn is
difficult to say. The canvas has also been given the
name *Picture of Human Life,* in view of the fragile
soap-bubbles which the child by the attic-window is
blowing. But there is no guarantee of the correctness
of this title either. As was often the case, Jan Steen has composed an interior
here from components which could never have existed side by side in reality.
Several figures are members of his family.

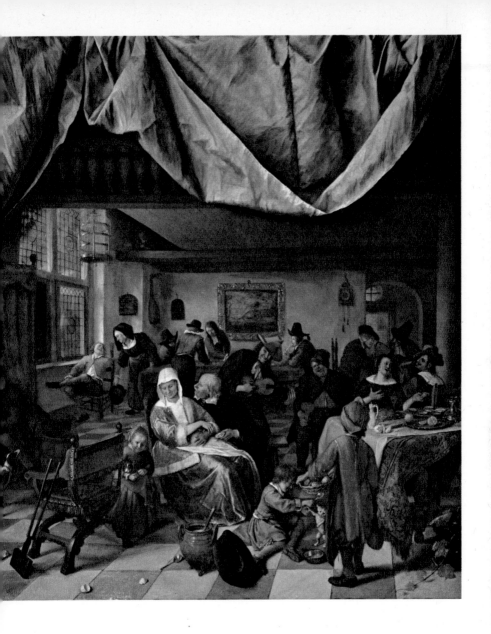

From the sales of A. Bout (The Hague, 11th August 1733) and Benjamin da Costa (The Hague, 13th August 1764), where it was bought for the cabinet of Prince William V.

JAN HAVICKSZ STEEN (1626–1679)
THE LUTE PLAYER   Panel
Mauritshuis No. 779   Height 31 cm. (12¹/₄″)
                                                          Width 27.5 cm. (10³/₄″)

His wife, his parents and his children were Jan Steen's principal models. Their characteristic figures can be seen over and over again (with that of the artist himself) in his interiors, eating, laughing, playing. Here Steen's wife alone is the subject, for once not depicted in a furnished room but posing before a neutral background. Grietje was the daughter of the land-scape-painter Jan van Goyen. She was born in 1639 and probably died in 1669. The portrait suggests that she may have been musical, as indeed were her husband and many of his Dutch fellow-artists of the seventeenth century. One often sees musical instruments in Steen's paintings. In fact there exists a self-portrait in which he himself plays the lute (Thyssen-Bornemisza Collection, Lugano). It is not a direct counterpart to this beauti-ful female musician but belongs to the same groups of works.

The portrait of Grietje Steen is of exquisite subtlety, both as regards its careful finishing-touches – almost like a miniature – and the well-chosen tasteful colouring whose subdued tones harmonise so splendidly with one another. Jan Steen came from Leyden, the town where, under the lead of Gerard Dou, the art of detailed painting was carried to its greatest heights, and after leaving his place of birth, he did not abandon the manner he had been taught there. Time and time again, between works of a more forceful character, he returned to his more detailed manner. These were often his most subtle and also his most witty pieces. As already mentioned, his family was a source of permanent inspiration to him.

The beautiful *Lute player* is from the sale of G. Smith (London, 1880), then in the P. J. Heseltine Collection, London, and a Dutch private col-lection. Exhibited from 1919 in the Mauritshuis which bought it in 1928.

JAN HAVICKSZ STEEN (1626–1679)

THE PARROT'S CAGE

Rijksmuseum No. 2245

Canvas on Panel

Height 50 cm. (19⁵/₈″)

Width 40 cm. (15³/₄″)

The Parrot's Cage shows, literally, the 'Jan Steen household' but this time it is not one of those untidy, noisy households which, rather unjustifiably, are thought to be typical of Steen's work, but a calm, orderly interior with well-to-do people. The artist has combined his colours with amazing craftsmanship. Those in the centre form an unexpected, piquant combination and are of a refinement which recalls the previous generation of Mannerists; the mauve jacket of the young woman, the pure white of her apron and the greenish-blue of her many-shaded silk skirt, placed before a grey wall against which the grey-black costume of the dice-player beside her contrasts demurely. Steen was a painter who, without surrendering his personality, was always open to the influences of others. Full colours like the red-brown of the Turkish table cloth and the jacket of the woman to the left baking oysters on the fire and the hues of the cheerful boy with the cat on the floor (he was undoubtedly Steen's own son) belong, however, to the generation of the Baroque.

No meaning or story should be looked for in this painting. Its virtues lie in the picturesque beauty of the interior, without further *arrière-pensée*. As a source of information about the seventeenth-century it is probably only of small value. As in *The Inn* in the Mauritshuis (page 233) the various components are in themselves undoubtedly realistic but the combination of the kitchen fire with the sculptured little gateway on the left, the parrot cage in the middle and the backgammon-players to the right, with a large bed in the background, obviously existed only in the artist's imagination. These are all things which Steen often depicted in his paintings.

The painting comes from the Lormier sale (The Hague, 1763) and the Van Heteren Cabinet at The Hague. In 1809 it was bought for the Rijksmuseum.

PIETER DE HOOCH (1629–1683 or after)

THE PANTRY   Canvas

Rijksmuseum No. 1248   Height 65   cm. (25⁵/₈″)

Width 60.5 cm. (23⁷/₈″)

With all their intimacy, the interiors of Pieter de Hooch always have
something spacious about them. This is because as a rule he did not confine
the painting to a single room but showed a view into others or the garden
or street through open doors or windows. It seems probable that the painter
had never seen such interiors in reality but composed them in his studio,
like his contemporary, Vermeer. *The Pantry* is an example of this combination of adjoining rooms. The effect of perspective is subtly reinforced
by the way in which the tiles of the first room are differently laid from
those in the second. The woman in the foreground may be De Hooch's
wife, Annetje van der Burch. The child to whom she passes a jug is their
eldest son Pieter, born in 1655. Here he is about three years old and therefore still clad in 'long clothes'. In the seventeenth century boys used to
wear skirts until their sixth year, a custom which still exists on the island
of Marken. The sleeves of the doublet and the collar, however, were
different for boys and girls so that we can tell this was in fact a boy. The
two streamers hanging from his shoulders are probably tapes used in learning to walk.

I am always inclined to think that the portrait decorating the wall in
the room adjoining the street, is of the painter's father and that Pieter de
Hooch, proud of his little son and heir, wanted to make a sort of family
piece of *The Pantry*. It should be admitted, however, that no definite
proof for this has yet been found.

The piece was painted about 1658 when De Hooch was still working in
Delft. The architecture of the interior is still simple. The warm ruddy tone
which predominates accentuates this unpretentious, bourgeois, but intimate
scene. Later, after he moved to Amsterdam, De Hooch was to direct his
attention towards the luxurious houses of the well-to-do in Holland's
Golden Age. *The Pantry* appeared at the sales of Pieter van der Lip
(Amsterdam, 1712), I. Walraven (Amsterdam, 1763), J. J. de Bruyn (Amsterdam, 1798), P. de Smeth van Alphen (Amsterdam, 1810) and Mrs
Hogguer (Amsterdam, 1817). Bought by the Rijksmuseum.

PIETER DE HOOCH (1629–1683 or after)

THE SMALL COUNTRY HOUSE
Rijksmuseum No. 1251

Canvas

Height 61 cm. (24″)
Width 47 cm. (18¹/₂″)

When Pieter de Hooch moved from Delft to Amsterdam he began to concentrate his interest on the richer section of society. In the long run this did not always benefit his art for the painter could not always guard against the attraction of excessive riches, excessive refinement. In his *Small Country House* in the Rijksmuseum, this is, however, not yet the case. This canvas must have been painted about 1665, therefore some two or three years after the artist had come to Amsterdam. It is still entirely in accordance with his Delft style but introduces different figures and objects.

We see a well-to-do couple chatting comfortably on a sunny summer's day in the shade of a bush. The man is smoking a pipe, the woman squeezing a lemon into a goblet of Rhine wine. Uninterested in the chatter of the two, a girl in the background scours a copper pan over the rain-butt. But another woman with a glass in her hand is obviously greatly interested in the conversation. This scene may be a latter-day rendering of the old theme of the 'five senses'. The combination of two rich and two simple figures is noteworthy.

The house that closes off the background is low and small but built in the 'grand style' with stately natural-stone pilasters which contrast sharply with the fresh red bricks of the walls. It is too beautiful for a farm but too small for an aristocratic country-house in the Beemster country or alongside the river Vecht. It possibly represents a building in one of the gardens which at the time were situated close under the walls of Amsterdam, in the Diemer polder or a little farther away, near Sloten. With its gay, bright colouring, its fine compositions of people with a house and garden and its successful combination of respectability and simplicity, the *Small Country House* is one of De Hooch's most cheerful and harmonious works.

The painting belonged to the Chaplin Collection (England). At the O'Neil sale in 1832 it was bought by the collector A. van der Hoop of Amsterdam who in 1854 bequeathed it to the city of Amsterdam. Lent to the Rijksmuseum in 1885.

JOHANNES VERMEER (1632–1675)
The Cook   Canvas
Rijksmuseum No. 2527 A 1   Height 45.5 cm. (17⁷/₈")
                                                   Width 41   cm. (16¹/₈")

Netherlandish painters did not show figures engaged in different work in
order to obtain a 'snapshot' effect. During the Renaissance they were more
interested in the intellectual side of a picture, while after it, due to their
purely aesthetic aims, they changed from humanists into painters. It was
their great talent which made possible this development and saved the
Dutch from an artistic impasse. For the Renaissance had aimed at a synthesis
of art and intellect but after a short period when the ideal appeared to have
been reached, painting threatened to degenerate into pseudo-learning, into
a thoughtless repetition of subjects of earlier days.

The Cook is indisputably the most noble product of this triumph of art
over pure intellect. It seems hard to connect it with the theme of the five
senses. The painting itself does not seem to have any particular meaning.
Vermeer has depicted the cook with wonderful concentration. She is
completely absorbed in her work, pouring out milk from a simple, red-
glazed jug into an earthenware pot. The rendering of the various substances
is outstanding: the creamy quality of the milk, the crumbly nature of the
bread on the table, definitely no longer fresh, the dry rushes of the basket in
the foreground, the hard gleaming surface of the Nassau stone pitcher, the
shining scoured yellow copper of the receptacle on the wall. The painting
is amazingly detailed. All the stains, the holes and the nail in the whitewashed background have been painted in order to avoid monotony.
Viewing it as a whole this is a gay scene, with blue, green, yellow, violet,
pink, brownish and brick-red and white in various strengths, combining in
a nuanced harmony.

The canvas dates from about 1658. It is mentioned at Amsterdam sales on
16th May 1696, and on 20th April 1701. Subsequently in the J. van Hoek
Collection at Amsterdam, in 1719; the P. L. de Neufville Collection,
Amsterdam, 1765; J. J. de Bruyn, Amsterdam, 1798; H. Muilman, Amsterdam, 1813; J. Six Collection. Bought by the Rijksmuseum in 1908.

242

JOHANNES VERMEER (1632–1675)

Young Girl   Canvas

Mauritshuis No. 670   Height 46.5 cm. (18$^1/_4$")

                                                   Width 40 cm. (15$^3/_4$")

Only a few of Vermeer's paintings are left, no more than about thirty. Possibly many of his works perished in the explosion which in 1654 destroyed a whole district of Delft. But the principal reason why his art is rare must lie in the fact that he worked very slowly. Vermeer's compositions have all been built up with extreme attention to detail. Nothing has been left to chance. The placing of the figures, colour, the light, rendering of the materials and, not to be forgotten, sometimes the emptiness of the backgrounds, is all thought out in an exceedingly detailed manner. The *Young Girl* in the Mauritshuis in its sober simplicity is an exception to Vermeer's work in general. As far as we know, he made only one other study of a head: the young woman looking back, from the Duke of Arenberg collection. According to Dr A. B. de Vries, 'no Dutch painter ever honoured woman as he did'. Vermeer's women are usually placed in interiors and are presented full-length, seen either full- or three-quarter-face.

It is not known who this girl was or the artist's 'intention' in painting her. I stress this question deliberately because Vermeer was never interested in picturesque qualities alone. In this case, however, nothing reminds us of this or that story, of allegory or symbolism. A soft shimmer of light is caught in the dark. A simple colour contrast; blue beside yellow, stands out against the obscure background. It is the play of light glimmering in the pearl which decorates her ear, more softly repeated by the two great, moist eyes and, once again, fleetingly, by the smile on the lower lip. Thus for us Vermeer's *Young Girl* is nothing but pure beauty, but very great beauty.

The painting is signed at the top but not dated. It is assumed that it originated about 1660. It was sold in Amsterdam on 16th May 1696. It then disappears from view until 1882 when Mr Braam of The Hague sold it to A. A. des Tombe of that town who bequeathed the piece in 1903 to the Mauritshuis.

JOHANNES VERMEER (1632–1675)

THE LITTLE STREET
Rijksmuseum No. 2527 A 2

Canvas
Height 54.3 cm. (21³/₈″)
Width 44 cm. (17³/₈″)

The old quarters of Delft today no longer contain the little façades which Vermeer depicted so magically, for in about 1660 they were demolished to make room for a new building for the Delft St Luke's Guild completed in 1661. According to P. T. A. Swillens, Vermeer shows the rear view of the Old Women's Home on the Volders Canal. The façades of the late-Gothic brick house on the right belongs to a type which still exists, especially in Gelderland and Westphalia, as well as in Utrecht. The lower part of the building has been whitewashed. But the closed shutters over the lower windows have not been touched for years and the paint on them has become drab-green and shabby. The small window panes are set in lead. In the open doorway sits a woman doing needlework. Near the simple wooden bench before the house two children are playing in the street. What the game is, we cannot see, possibly knucklebones. In the passage between the houses another woman bends over the butt of rain water. Beside her stands a broom which suggests that she is drawing water to scrub the street. The small, yellow paving-bricks look spotlessly clean.

Against the house to the left, of which we can only see half (it is the Old Men's Home), grows a vine. The green of the leaves has separated because the blue paint which Vermeer mixed in it has almost completely eliminated the yellow, but the fine, pale tone which now characterises the canvas is such that one cannot regret the change.

The painting must have originated about 1658. In a sale of 1696 another similar piece by Vermeer, *A View of Some Houses* is mentioned, but this can no longer be traced.

First mentioned at an Amsterdam auction on 16th May 1696. Then in the collections of G. W. Oosten de Bruyn (Amsterdam, 1800), Van Winter (Amsterdam) and Six (until 1921). Donated to the Rijksmuseum by Sir Henry Deterding.

JOHANNES VERMEER (1632–1675)
VIEW OF DELFT   Canvas
Mauritshuis No. 92
Height 98.5 cm. (38⁷/₈″)
Width 117.5 cm. (46¹/₄″)

This view of Delft is from the south.
The river is the Schie, which here is
called the Kolkje and extends past the
bridge into the town. On either side of
the bridge a gate breaks the continuity
of the town-wall. The one on the left is
the Schiedam Gate; the other the Rotterdam Gate. Behind the latter is the tower
of the New Church. Behind and to the
left of the Schiedam Gate is the Munitions
Store of Holland.

The painter viewed this panorama
from a fair distance. He was separated
from it by the yellowish, sandy quay in
the foreground. On the second plane is
the expanse of water and behind it Delft.
All the elements of the picture are
painted in extraordinary detail. Everything is dominated by an indefinable
atmosphere. The diffuse light mingles
with the very warm tones. And the
darkest parts of the town are reflected
even darker in the softly rippling water.

The painting must have originated
about 1658. It was sold at an Amsterdam auction on 16th May 1696. Next
at the Stinstra sale (Amsterdam, 22nd
May 1822); bought there for the Mauritshuis.

248

JOHANNES VERMEER (1632–1675)

THE LETTER   Canvas

Rijksmuseum No. 2528   Height 44 cm. (17^3/$_8$")

                                            Width 38.5 cm. (15^1/$_4$")

Like other pictures by Vermeer, this one shows the interior of the artist's house, but composed according to the rules and refinements of Baroque. In the first room hangs a map of North Holland while on the right stands a chair on which lies a pile of music paper. A handwoven carpet (perhaps made in Delft?) has been draped back to reveal the next room. The latter is clearly lighted but one cannot see the windows as they are behind the wall to the left. This device of hiding the sources of light was much used by Baroque painters. Oblique lines running from the foreground to the background link the two rooms: the broom standing behind the chair against the wall, the two slippers beside it and, especially, the black and white marble tiles laid in a zig-zag pattern. In the second room, in full light, a lady looks up from her lute-playing and exchanges a few words with a maid who has just brought her a letter. The play of light, perspective and even the iconography lead the eye easily from the foreground to the second plane. Nothing is left to chance: the gaze passes from the chair in the dark room to the seated lady, and the letter forms the centre of the second plane. On closer examination, the picture reveals all sorts of exquisite details: the wonderful play of colours which have been preserved in incredibly fresh condition, the small yet pronounced highlights on the black broom and the white pearl on the ear of the lady, the brilliant red of the maid's lips, the piece of beautiful brocade which has been hung along the whitewashed wall, the blue sewing box and the laundry basket on the floor, just touched by light.

These components, in all their richness and multiplicity, have been combined into a perfect unity. The painting must have originated about 1666. It is possibly identical with a work which was sold on 16th May 1696 at Amsterdam. Later it belonged to the J. F. van Lennep Collection at Amsterdam. Messchert van Vollenhoven sale, Amsterdam, 1892. Acquired for the Rijksmuseum in 1893 by the Rembrandt Society.

250

FRANS VAN MIERIS (1635–1681)
THE SOLDIER AND THE GIRL   Panel
Mauritshuis No. 860   Height 43 cm. (16⁷/₈")
                                                         Width 33 cm. (13")

Not only is this a finely painted panel by the artist who in the third
quarter of the seventeenth century was the leading master of the Leyden
School, but also a picture with a moral story – rather like that of the
Prodigal Son. The work is dated 1659. It has been described by Dr H.
Gerson as fellows; 'The daring subject has received witty treatment. The
visitors and the contents of the room leave no doubt as to the subject of
the picture. But really the subject here is less relevant than the seductive and
fascinating manner of painting. Who else has ever so completely and so
subtly harmonised the colours of a painting with the silver lustre of silk?
The technique is perfect, according to the best Leyden recipe, without being
boring. The still-life of lute and jug against the white wall recalls Vermeer
although Frans van Mieris was probably not following Vermeer's example.
Van Mieris' later works often regress into the Leyden smoothness and into
superficial technical refinement but about 1635–60 he was, with Metsu, an
important figure in Dutch painting.'

Another version of this picture, with variants, was in the Nostitz Gallery
at Prague. All his life Frans van Mieris worked in his birthplace, Leyden.
He learnt painting from Gerard Dou and Abraham van den Tempel. He
had a fairly profound influence on the next generation, especially on his
sons Frans and Willem but neither of these reached the heights of their
father.

Lent by the Rijksdienst voor's Roerend Kunstbezit to the Mauritshuis
in 1948.

MELCHIOR D'HONDECOETER (1636–1695)

<small>THE MENAGERY</small>   Canvas
Rijksmuseum No. 1223   Height 135 cm. (53¹/₈")
                                                  Width 116.5 cm. (34³/₄")

D'Hondecoeter painted this decorative piece for the palace of Soestdijk,
which Prince William III had bought and had had rebuilt and decorated by
various artists. Most important was d'Hondecoeter, then reputed to be the
best painter of live birds in the Netherlands. Even today his pictures are
unrivalled of their kind. In his town garden at Amsterdam he kept a small
menagery, as did the Prince too at Soestdijk. During the French Revolution
this canvas, with other, was removed from Soestdijk to the National Art
Gallery collection, the predecessor of the Rijksmuseum.

JAN VAN HUYSUM (1682–1749)
FLOWERS AND FRUIT   Panel
Rijksmuseum No. 1274   Height 81 cm. (31⁷/₈″)
                                            Width 61 cm. (24″)

While Ambrosius Bosschaert's art heralded the flowerpiece, Jan van Huysum's work followed on a long development. In his colouring the painter
aimed more and more at light, airy effects, in accordance with the taste of
the eighteenth century. This was his greatest innovation. In this still-life the
process had only just begun, so that it must date from the first years of the
eighteenth century. His flower-pieces influenced painters throughout Europe.
The panel was donated by Mrs Messchert van Vollenhoven-van Lennep
of Amsterdam to the city which in 1892 lent it tŏ the Rijksmuseum.

CORNELIS TROOST (1697–1750)
BLIND MAN'S BUFF   Canvas
Boymans-van Beuningen Museum No. 447 a   Height 68 cm. (26³/₄")
                                                Width 74 cm. (29¹/₈")

Troost was greatly influenced by stage design and the theatre, which provided the subjects of many of his pastels. This links him with such French
artists as Guillot, Watteau, Lancret and Pater, although he was not directly
influenced by them. Troost's game takes place in the garden of a country
residence, perhaps beside the river Amstel, although the scenery is more like
a decor for an operetta with figures in elegant and colourful dress—for an
amateur performance in which, despite the best intentions, the necessary
speed and refinement are just lacking. Bought by the museum in 1939 aided
by the Rembrandt Society.

CORNELIS TROOST (1697–1750)

ALEXANDER THE GREAT IN THE BATTLE OF THE GRANICUS   Canvas
Rijksmuseum No. 2326   Height 110   cm. (43¹/₄″)
                                      Width 132.5 cm. (52¹/₄″)

Troost was one of those who practised the 'grand style' which was much
more fashionable in the Netherlands than many of us realise today. The
'historical piece' with classical content evoked heroic ideals much admired
at the time in literature and in the theatre as well. According to the art-
historian J. Knoef, Troost did not merely take over the clichés of French
classical painting. His *Alexander the Great in the Battle of the Granicus*
shows characteristics peculiar to him: ingenuity of composition, thorough
technique and fine colour and treatment of light. The work is a good
example of Dutch 'classicism'. The painting is dated 1737. It appeared
at the H. Muilman sales (Amsterdam, 1813) and was in 1880 bequeathed
by Jonkheer J. S. H. van de Poll to the Rijksmuseum.

TAKO JELGERSMA (1702–1795)
PORTRAITS OF ALBERT AND HENDRIK FABRICIUS AS CHILDREN   Pastels
each Height 34 cm. (13³/₈″)
Frans Hals Museum Nos. 178 and 179   Width 29 cm. (11³/₈″)

The name of this painter has been forgotten amid the overwhelming riches of excellent artists whom the seventeenth century Netherlands had at their disposal. But in many a foreign town a master of his qualities would have remained honoured. His pastel portraits of the Fabricius boys, sons of Willem Fabricius of Haarlem are attractive cabinet-pieces. The elder – in 1748 when he was painted, he was twelve years old – was already turning into a gentleman, a young ruler in miniature. On his self-assured little face we read the self-will of a far from easy personality. He must have been spoiled, used to a lot of servants who saw to his fashionable curls and where at his beck and call. The younger brother – he was only ten years old – seems of a more impulsive nature; perhaps he was quick-tempered. Both are elegantly dressed as though they were adults. Notwithstanding, these are charming children's portraits.

In 1883 they were bequeathed from family property by Jonkheer J. C. W. Fabricius van Leyenburg to the Frans Hals Museum.

258

TIBOUT REGTERS (1710–1768)

JAN BRAK AND HIS FAMILY

Rijksmuseum No. 2014 A 3

Canvas

Height 67.5 cm. (26½″)
Width 84 cm. (33⅛″)

The atmosphere into which Tibout Regters leads us differs strongly from that of his contemporary Jelgersma. He shows us that besides the rich and proud ruling families, there were also living in Holland wealthy people who led quieter and simpler lives. The minister seated on the left is the son, Jan Brak, since 1743 a teacher in the Baptist community. Through the open door one sees the library. The father, Herman Brak, sits in the centre of the group. Cornelis is on the right, with his wife Margaretha Hasselaar and their two children. The English call eighteenth-century family groups of this type 'conversation pieces'. The genre originated in the seventeenth century, however, in the Netherlands. In 1904 Miss C. M. Bakker of Baarn gave this painting to the Rijksmuseum.

JEAN BAPTISTE SIMÉON CHARDIN (1699–1779)

GRACE BEFORE THE MEAL   Canvas

Boymans-van Beuningen Museum   Height 50.5 cm. (19³/₄″)

                                           Width 66.5 cm. (26¹/₄″)

The art of the 'bourgeois' subject which the Le Nain brothers had practised in the seventeenth century (see page 166) was continued in eighteenth-century France by Chardin. That he was inspired by the Flemish school appears clearly from a note on a picture sent to the Paris Salon of 1746: 'Un tableau, répétition du Bénédicté, avec addition, pour faire pendant à un Teniers, placé dans le cabinet de M. de la Live.' Five years afterwards he exhibited the same work in the Salon; it was then described as 'répétition du tableau, qui est au Cabinet du Roi, mais avec des changements.' A drawing in the Salon catalogue of 1761, which belonged to Gabriel de Saint-Aubin (now in the Cabinet des Estampes, Paris), proves that the canvas exhibited then is identical with the one now hanging in the Rotterdam museum.

Chardin did not only imitate Teniers. He adapted Teniers' pictorial ideas to suit French taste. The craftsmen, the alchemists and the peasants were replaced by the lower middle classes. He replaced good-natured Flemish exuberance with a subtle good taste and often with elegance. The colouring became lighter and more delicate. Bu the most important thing was that his great talent made of every subject, which in other hands might easily have inclined towards anecdote, a warmly human picture, without however lapsing in the process into the pathetic or sentimental. So Chardin became the great master of what is intimate. He did not overload his paintings with dramatic, theatrical or heroic-effects. It is curious to realise that this painter worked in the Paris of the period of the frivolous regency of the Duc d'Orleans and of the over-refined culture of the Court of Louis XV and Madame de Pompadour. All this life went past him, living in his rather isolated house in the Faubourg Saint-Germain. He concentrated his whole attention on still-lifes of simple, sometimes very beautiful but never really precious things (here, too, the Dutch painters influenced him). He chose as his subjects children and happy mothers, simple but never poor interiors. He shows us in this paintings one particular facet of French life, and thanks to his art, this can attract our interest and our sympathy. Only a later generation was to discover all this and to learn how to appreciate at its value the sublime qualities of Chardin's work.

The painting comes from the collection of De La Live, Paris; a lawyer called Forier (from 1761, auctioned 2nd April 1770); Choiseul-Pranslin

(sale of 8th February 1793); Charlier; Camille Marcille (about 1860–1887); Eudoxe Marcille; Sir Robert Abdy, Paris, and D. G. van Beuningen, Vierhouten, Holland. With his collection it was in 1958 acquired by the Rotterdam Museum.

JEAN BAPTISTE PERRONNEAU (1715–1783)
PORTRAIT OF SARA HINLOOPEN   Pastel on Parchment
Rijksmuseum No. 2951 B 3   Height 58.5 cm. (23″)
                                                 Width 46 cm. (18¹/₈″)

In the eighteenth century several prominent French portraitists tried their luck in the Netherlands. Perroneau travelled there frequently, in 1754 going for the first time to The Hague where there were more Francophiles at the Court than anywhere else in the country. Only later was he also to find a *clientèle* in Amsterdam; but during a third visit to the Republic in March 1763 he made portraits of Arent van der Waeyen (1684–1767), a prosperous businessman and former governor, who was then already seventy-eight years of age, and his wife, Sara Hinloopen. She was then seventy-four; she had a toothless, mumbling mouth, her cheeks were fallen in, the flesh had become flabby and her expression vacant. Or did she still have keen eyes and is her face only marked by boredom as a result of the long sitting? Her hair has obviously not yet been arranged. Her dress is hidden from view by a négligé of flowered Indian damask and a wide neckerchief.

The pastel is as vivid in drawing as in colour. The fine light blue of the dressing-gown and the white of the scarf and cap frame the pink face. The portrait is extraordinarily human; whether Sara Hinloopen had an amiable character is a different question. The painter portrayed his models uncompromisingly as he saw them. His concern was that his portrait should accurately reflect his sitter's personality. His patrons seem to have accepted this, as, somewhat later, Goya's patrons did also. Certainly many citizens of Amsterdam had themselves painted by him in 1763.

By inheritance the portrait of Sara Hinloopen, with that of her husband, came into the possession of the Van Lynden family. In 1950 the Rijksmuseum bought it from Baron van Lynden van Horstwaerde.

JEAN ETIÉNNE LIOTARD (1702–1789)
LANDSCAPE NEAR GENEVA   Pastel on Parchment
Rijksmuseum No. 2949
Height 45 cm. (17³/₄")
Width 58 cm. (22⁷/₈")

Liotard's art is best represented in the museums
of Geneva and Amsterdam. These are the two
towns that meant most to the artist. Geneva
was his birth place, Amsterdam the city where
he met his future wife. Later he returned to
Switzerland after travels throughout Europe
and it was there he painted his own portrait,
modestly tucked away in a corner, a drawing
pencil in his hand, a red bonnet on the sleek
grey hair, looking out from his studio at the
landscape before him (as it says on the back
of the pastel). It is a gay, sunny summer's day.
A vine is growing in the garden in the foreground. Behind in the meadows the dry
yellow hay lies on the land. Further away cows
are grazing and a man drives two black horses
before the plough. Even farther off are some
houses among trees and behind them rise the
mountains, first low, then high and snow-
covered. The blue sky above gleams in a even
expanse. An inexpressible calm pervades this
peaceful landscape. This pastel reflects that
love of nature which Liotard felt at the end
of his life.

It remained in the possession of the Liotard
family until Miss M. A. Liotard bequeathed
it in 1873 to the Rijksmuseum.

PIERRE PAUL PRUD'HON (1758–1823)
RUTGER JAN SCHIMMELPENNINCK AND HIS FAMILY   Canvas
Rijksmuseum No. 1923 c   Height 263.5 cm. (103³/₄")
                                           Width 200 cm. (78³/₄")

The great portrait of Schimmelpenninck and his family is amongst the most arresting that Prud'hon painted. It is cool in tone, reserved in character, and despite its large size, the composition is harmonious and lacks the unattractive colouring of his later works, which conformed to the taste of his time. When he painted the Ambassador Schimmelpenninck in 1801 or 1802, the artist had achieved a mastery of his style. He had rejected the hard rigid lines of classicism, its heavy colour and its monumental type of composition. Romanticism had not yet influenced him, so that at the age of forty, Prud'hon was at the peak of his abilities.

The same can be said of Rutger Jan Schimmelpenninck (1761–1825). He had not been born into the old ruling class and so had not been destined for public office. After the completion of his law studies he established himself in Amsterdam as a lawyer. The French Revolution inspired this intelligent young man with progressive ideas. He was swiftly successful. He became the Ambassador in Paris and then in London in 1802, in the same year representing his country at the Peace Conference of Amiens. Napoleon had sympathy for this worthy man whose modern ideas were tempered by humanity and prudence, and in 1805 nominated him Grand Pensionary of the Batavian Republic. He resigned this office in 1806, however, when Louis Bonaparte became King of Holland. A cataract compelled him to leave public life.

Schimmelpenninck's small son Gerrit (1794–1863), who in the painting is playing happily with a deer, followed a career worthy of his father. He became a prominent diplomat and banker, director of the *Netherlands Handelmaatschappij* and, in 1848, Prime Minister. His sister Catherina, whom we see on Prud'hon's canvas standing on the left, was later to go to London as the wife of the Dutch ambassador Salomon Dedel.

The portrait group was exhibited in the Paris Salon of 1802. Until 1929 it remained the property of the Ambassador's descendants. In that year it was donated by Mr and Mrs Drucker-Fraser to the Rijksmuseum.

PIETER RUDOLPH KLEYN (17ᴊ5–1816)

VIEW IN THE PARK OF SAINT CLOUD

Canvas
Height 99 cm. (39")

Rijksmuseum No. 1351

Width 130 cm. (51¹/₈")

Louis Bonaparte, who in 1806 was made King of Holland by his powerful brother, the Emperor Napoleon, took great trouble over the prosperity of his kingdom. He was also a patron of the arts who enabled a number of promising young painters and architects to study in Paris and Rome. In 1808, Pieter Rudolph Klein, aged twenty, left for France as a protegé of the King of Holland to put himself under the tuition of J. L. David. The year after his arrival at Paris he painted this *View in the Park of St Cloud*. The park is seen from the centre of the great avenue, at the time newly laid out by Le Notre, and still in existence today. One can recognise the place easily, for since 1809 little has been changed. In the distance is the Pont de Sèvres; on the left the banks of the Seine, now marred by sheds. The stately high trees have in the course of time been replaced by others which, however, stand in the same places and look as fine as those that Kleyn painted.

The colouring of the landscape is forceful but at the same time some-what diffuse. Nowhere does it show the strong, hard tones one so often finds in David's work. There is no evidence at all here of his influence on his pupil. One would rather be inclined to call the *View in the Park of Saint Cloud* Romantic. Its shapes and planes, the play of light, and the colours recall the Empire style. Kleyn has here painted a delicate and dreamy work. In the years 1808–1809 our artist painted yet other landscapes in the environs of Paris, but this clear view is one of his best works. The painting was included in an exhibition in 1810 at the Royal Palace, Amsterdam, and was bought there for the Royal Museum, the predecessor of the Rijksmuseum.

FRANCISCO JOSE DE GOYA Y LUCIENTES (1746–1828)

PORTRAIT OF DON RAMON SATUE   Canvas
Rijksmuseum   Height 107   cm. (42¹/₈″)
                                                 Width   83.5 cm. (32³/₄″)

Goya often not only signed and dated his canvases but also mentioned
the name of the sitter. On Goya's canvas in the Rijksmuseum one reads
in the left lower corner 'D. Ramon Satue Akalde de Corte P. Goya 1823'.
The sitter was a judge in Madrid. Like Goya he was in favour of the
new liberal ideas, and they were both forced to take refuge when in
1823 the monarchist counter-revolution broke out. This portrait, then,
was painted in 1823. The grey background and gentle light suggest that
it was made indoors. The sitter is informally dressed, the collar of his
shirt open for comfort, the pleated jabot falls to the side, the black jacket
and the red waistcoat underneath have been carelessly arranged, look
creased and worn. His tangled hair is brushed forward and needs dressing.
No gentleman would show himself in the street like this. But Don
Ramon Satue is intensely alive here, for Goya has used all his skill as a
portraitist in painting him. The face reflects the spirit of revolution. Neither
he nor Goya were to accept dictatorship or the flattering styles which
followed the reign of Joseph Bonaparte. The portrait is not in keeping with
the official style of post-Napoleonic Spain. Goya was to leave his country
in 1824 to flee to Bordeaux, where he died four years later.

   This painting belonged to the collection of the Marquess de Heredia in
Madrid. In 1890 it was sold at the Benito Garriga sale in Paris, and entered
the possession of Dr J. Carvallo, near Tours, in 1902. In 1922 is was bought
by the Rijksmuseum with the help of the Rembrandt Society.

The letter in brackets which follows the title of each painting indicates the gallery in which it is hung:

B: Boymans-van Beuningen Museum

R: Rijksmuseum

M: Mauritshuis

H: Frans Hals Museum

Gérard David Madonna and
Child in a Landscape (B)

Bishopric of Liège Norfolk Triptych (B)

Master of Aix
The Prophet Isaiah (B)

Dirck Bouts
The Features of Christ (B)

Jan Provoost
The Dispute of St Catherine (B)

Hans Memlinc
Two Horses (B)

Quentin Matsys Madonna and Child (M)

Joachim Patinir Sodom and Gomorrah on Fire (B)

273

Geertgen tot St Jans
The Tree of Jesse (R)

Geertgen tot St Jans
Holy Family and their Kindred (R)

Bosch Adoration of the Magi (B)

Master of Virgo inter Virgines
Annunciation (B)

Master of the Death of the Virgin, Amsterdam
The Death of the Virgin (R)

Jan Mostaert
A Prophet (B)

Geertgen tot St Jans
The Virgin in Majesty

Jacob Cornelisz van Oostsanen
Mount Calvary (R)

Lucas van Leyden
The Sermon (R)

Master of Spes Nostra
Allegory of the Vanity of Human Life (R)

Master of Delft Triptych (R)

Hieronymus Bosch Two Wings from a Triptych with Parables

Jan Mostaert The Discovery of America

Master of Alkmaar The Seven Works of Charity

Antonio Moro
Portrait of a Goldsmith (M)

Maerten van Heemskerck
Portrait of a Man (B)

Jan Mostaert
Portrait of a Lady (R)

Jan van Scorel The Baptism of Christ (H)

Jan van Scorel St Mary Magdalen (R)

Jan van Scorel Crusaders at Haarlem (H)

Pieter Aertsz Jesus at the House of Martha and Mary (B)

Dürer The Holy Family (B)   *Holbein* Elisabeth Schmid (M) *Master of the Life of Mary*
The Visitation (B)

Adriaen Isenbrandt   *Bernard van Orley* Christ Crucified   *Aert Pietersz* Portrait of a Lady (R)
Madonna and Child (B)   between the Virgin and St John

Cornelis Anthonisz Banquet of the Civic Guard in Amsterdam (R)

277

Fra Angelico
Virgin and Child (R)

Josaphat Araldi Ariadne (R)

Veronese The Disciples at Emmaus (B)

Pellegrino Tibaldi The Visitation (R)

Giorgione Allegory of Chastity (R)

Botticelli Judith (R)

Ambrogio Borgnone
Virgin and Child (R)

Ercole de Roberti
Portrait of Pietro Cenni (B)

Dosso Dossi
Mythological Scene (B)

Giambattista Moroni
Portrait of a Lady (R)

Pontormo Portrait of a Lady (R)

Bernardo Strozzi David (B)

Titian Child in a Landscape (B)

Tintoretto The Woman taken in Adultery (R)

Giambattista Moroni
Portrait of a Camaldolensian Monk (B)

Jordaens
The Adoration of the Shepherds (M)

Rubens
Portrait of Michel Ophovius (M)

Rubens Diana Bathing (B)

Jordaens The Coin in the Mouth of a Fish (R)

Jordaens Satyr (R)

Van Dyck Portrait of a Lady (M)

Van Dyck William II and
Princess Mary Stuart (R)

Jan Fyt Still-life (B)

Velvet Brueghel Flower-piece (R)

Rubens
Portrait of a Carmelite Monk (B)

Rubens
Thetis dips Achilles in the Styx (B)

Rubens St Livinus' Martyrdom (B)

Rubens The Three Crosses (B)

Rubens The Assumption (M)

Rubens and Jan Brueghel Adam and Eve in Paradise (M)

David Teniers The Alchemist (M)

281

Cornelisz van Haarlem The Wedding of Pelée and Thetis (H)

Abraham Bloemaert
The Lamentation of Christ (B)

Vermeer Diana and her Companions (M)

Jean-Baptiste de Champaigne and Nicholas de Plattemontagne
Portrait of the Two Artists (B)

Velazquez Still-life (R)

Greco Christ Crucified (R)

Pieter Lastman Flight into Egypt (B)

282

Frans Hals The Meagre Company (R)

Frans Hals
Portrait of Jacob Olycan (M)

Frans Hals Banquet of the Officers of the Civic Guard
of St George at Haarlem (H)

Frans Hals Marie Voogt (R)

Jan de Bray The Governors of the Children's
Home (H)

283

Frans Hals Assembly of Officers and Subalterns
of St Adrian at Haarlem (H)

Frans Hals Officers and Subalterns of St George
at Haarlem (H)

Frans Hals
Portrait of Lucas de Clerq (R)

Fans Hals Portrait of N. Hasselaer (R)

Frans Hals
Portrait of an Old Lady (B)

Frans Hals The Governors of St Elizabeth's Hospital
at Haarlem (H)

Willem Buytewech Merry Company (B)

284

Jan de Bray Christ blessing the Children (H)   *Fieter Fransz de Grebber* The Works of Charity (H)

Jan de Bray Portrait of a Boy (M)   *Molenaer* Lady at the Harpsichord (R)   *Jan Cornelisz Verspronck*
Portrait of a Girl (R)

Frans Hals The Governors of the Old Men's Home   *Frans Hals* The Lady Governors of the Old Men's Home
at Haarlem (H)   at Haarlem (H)

285

Willem Claesz Heda Still-life (R)

Pieter Claesz Still-life (R)

Jan Jansz van de Velde Still-life (R)

Jan Davidsz de Heem Still-life with Books (M)

Van der Heyden Still-life (M)

Pieter Cornelisz van Rijck The Kitchen (R)

Pieter de Putter Still-life with Fish (H)   *Jan Davidsz de Heem*   *Melchior d'Hondecouter*
                                                  Flower-piece (R)   The Birds (R)

Ambrosius Bosschaert   *Balthasar van der Ast*   *Jan Weenix* Dead Game (R)
   Flowers (R)   Still-life with Shells (B)

Jan Davidsz de Heem Still-life with a Ham (B)   *Rachel Ruysch* Flower-piece (R)   *Jan van Huysum*
                                                                              Still-life with Flowers (R)

287

Frans van Mieris Portrait of
the Artist and his Wife (M)

Jan Steen
Girl with Oysters (M)

Gerard Dou
Self-portrait

Gerard Dou
Young Woman Dressing

Godfried Schalcken
Portrait of William III (R)

Gerard Dou The Charlatan (B)

Steen Adoration of the Shepherds (R)

Steen The Poultry-yard (M)

Jan Steen The Sick Lady (R)

Jan Steen The Prince's Birthday (R)

288

Self-portrait (R)   The Feast of St Nicholas (R)   The Dancing Lesson of a Cat (R)

The Disciples at Emmaus (R)   The Oysters (B)

Village Wedding (B)   The Merry Company (M)

289

Joseph telling his Dreams (R)   Simeon in the Temple (M)   The Lamentations of Jeremiah (R)

Rembrandt's Mother (R)   Titus in a Monk's Hood (R)   Portrait of Maria Trip (R)

The Anatomy Lesson of Professor Tulp (M)   Dead Peacocks (R)

Rembrandt Man in a Red Cap (B)

Hercules Seghers Landscape (R)

Rembrandt
Rembrandt's Brother (M)

Rembrandt Peace (B)

Rembrandt Two Negroes (M)

Rembrandt
Last Self-portrait (M)

Rembrandt Homer (M)

Rembrandt The Denial of St Peter (R)

291

Carel Fabritius Portrait
of Abraham de Potter (R)

Paudiss Still-life (B)

Govert Flinck
Isaac blessing Jacob (R)

Ferdinand Bol Portrait
of Roelof Meulenaer (R)

Jacob-Adriaensz Backer
Boy in Grey (M)

Aert de Gelder
Jehovah and the Angels with Abraham (B)

Nicholas Maes
Prayer without End (R)

Ferdinand Bol Lady with a Fan (B)

Ferdinand Bol Portrait
of Elizabeth Bas (R)

Ferdinand Bol
Governors of the Poor House

Ferdinand Bol
Portrait of Michel de Ruyter

PORTRAITS

Werner van den Valckert The Lady Governors (R)

Paulus Moreelse
'The Little Princess' (R)

Michiel Jansz van Miereveld
Portrait of Aegje Hasselaer (R)

Jacob I Willemsz Delff
Portrait of a Young Boy (R)

Michiel Jansz van Miereveld
Portrait of Prince Maurits

Bartholomeus van der Helst
Portrait of Andries Bicker (R)

Thomas de Keyser
Portrait of Loef Vredericx (M)

293

Bartholomeus van der Helst Banquet of the Civic Guard (R)

Bartholomeus van der Helst Young Couple (B)

Pieter van Anraadt Family Group on a Terrace (R)

Abraham Lambertsz van den Tempel
Jan van Amstel and his Wife (B)

Johannes de Baen
Portrait of Prince Johan Maurits

Hanneman Portraits of
Constant Huygens and his Children (M)

Bartholomeus van der Helst
Portrait of Princess Mary Stuart (R)

Pastor van der Schalcke (R)   Portrait of Helena van der Schalcke (R)   Portrait of Aletta Pancras (R)

Flagellant Procession (R)   Self-portrait (M)

Group in an Interior (R)   Portrait of Jacob de Graeft (R)   *Mozes ter Borch*
Portrait of a Young Man (R)

295

Gabriel Metsu The Sick Child (R)

Gabriel Metsu
The Sportsman's Present (R)

Vermeer The Letter (R)

De Witte Interior with a Lady at the Harpsichord (B)

Pieter de Hooch The Linen Cupboard (R)

Quiringh Gerritsz Brekelenkam
The Blood-letting (M)

Eglon van der Neer
A Lady washing her Hands (M)

Jan Verkolje The Message (M)

Pieter Jansz Saenredam
The Town Hall, Amsterdam (R)

Saenredam The Church at Assendelft (R)

Lieve de Jongh View of Rotterdam (B)

Emanuel de Witte The Fishmarket (R)

Job Berckheyde The Court of the
Old Exchange, Amsterdam (B)

Job Berckheyde St Bavon's Church (R)

Jan van der Heyden
The Martelaarsgracht, Amsterdam (R)

Jan van der Heyden
View of the Jesuit Church, Dusseldorf (M)

297

Hendrick Cornelisz Vroom Arrival at Vlessingen of the Count
Palatine Frederick V and his Wife Elizabeth (H)

Lieve Verschuier
Arrival of Charles II at Rotterdam (R)

Hendrick Cornelisz Vroom The Return from Brazil
of Paulus van Caerden (R)

Ludolf Bakhuysen The 'King William' (R)

Adam Willaerts The Meuse near Den Brie (B)

Willem van de Velde the Elder Council of
War on the 'Seven Provinces' (R)

Willem van de Velde the Elder Naval Battle at
Ter Heyde (R)

Willem van de Velde the Younger The Harbour
of Amsterdam (R)

LANDSCAPES

Adriaen Pietersz van de Venne The Horsemarket, Valkenburg (R)   *Jacob Jacobsz van Geel* Landscape (R)

Jan van Goyen River View (R)   *Arent Arentsz* Landscape with a Sportsman (R)

Salomon van Ruysdael River View (R)   *Jacob van Ruisdael*
Windmill near ' Wijk bij Duurstede ' (R)

Paul Potter The Young Bull (M)   *Aelbert Cuyp*
Landscape with Two Cows (R)   *Paul Potter*
Landscape with Cattle (R)

Adam Pynacker Landscape (R)

Hackaert
The Ash-tree Avenue (R)

Lingelbach Italian Harbour (R)

Frans Post Brazilian Landscape (R)

Philips Koninck Landscape (R)

Frans Post Tamaraca Island (M)

Berchem Cattle crossing a River (R)

Jan van Huysum Landscape (R)

Adriaen Beeldemaker The Sportsman (R)

Frédéric de Moucheron
Italian Landscape (R)

Tiepolo Telemachus (R)

Tiepolo Virgin and Child with
St John Baptist (R)

Giovanni Domenico Tiepolo
The Flight into Egypt (R)

Guardi View of the Brenta Canal, Venice (R)

Guardi The Grand Canal, Venice (B)

Alessandro Magnasco
Hermits in a Landscape (R)

Giovanni Battista Piazetta
The Fruit-Girl (R)

Giacomo Ceruti
Portrait of an Old Lady (R)

EIGHTEENTH-CENTURY
FRENCH AND ITALIAN PAINTERS

Watteau Indiscretion (B)

Jean-Baptiste Joseph Pater
Fête champêtre (B)

Hubert Robert The Painter's Studio (B)

Boucher Chinoiserie (B)

Vanvitelli View of Rome (R)

Chardin Still-life (B)

Pietro Longhi Masked Scene (R)

2

Family Group in an Interior (R)   Portrait of van der Mersch (R)   Town Garden (R)

The Brethren began to Talk (M)   There was a Noise in the House (M)

Portrait of Isaac Sweers (R)   The Wedding of Kloris and Roosje (M)   Portrait of Jan Lepeltak (R)

303

Joseph-Auguste Knip
Place de la Concorde (R)

Jean-Etienne Liotard Portrait of
Francesco Algarotti (R)

Frans van der Mijn
Portrait of a Lady (R)

Jacob de Wit Grisaille with Putti (R)

Van Troostwijk
The 'Raamportje', Amsterdam

Nicholaes Muys
The Lovers of Art (B)

Tischbein Portrait of
Wilhelmina of Prussia (R)

Jan Ekels the Younger
The Writer (R)

Hodges Portrait of
Louis-Napoleon (R)

Wybrand Hendriks The Notary
Köhne and his Clerk (R)

LIST OF ILLUSTRATIONS

Colour plates are indicated by the page numbers in italics.

305

311

313